CANADIAN SPORTS RECORDS

J. Alexander Poulton

Gary Queensway

OVER
TIME
BOOKS

The Publisher: OverTime Books is an imprint of Éditions de la
Montagne Verte

Library and Archives Canada Cataloguing in Publication

Queensway, Gary, 1980–
    Canadian sports records / Gary Queensway,
J. Alexander Poulton

Includes bibliographical references.
ISBN 978-1-897277-37-9

    1. Sports records—Canada. 2. Sports—Canada—History.
I. Poulton, J. Alexander (Jay Alexander), 1977– . II. Title.

GV585.Q44 2009   796.0971   C2008-906160-8

Project Director: J. Alexander Poulton
Project Editor: Carla MacKay
Production: HR Media Group
Cover Image: Courtesy of Fotosearch (OJO Images)

We acknowledge the financial support of the Government of
Canada through the Book Publishing Industry Development
Program for our publishing activities.

 Canadian   Patrimoine
Heritage   canadien

PC: 1

Dedication

To Grover, Winnie and Philip—you know
who wears the pants.

Contents

Introduction

Canada is widely known around the world for its skill and devotion to the game of hockey, but in the last century and then some, Canada has produced some of the most interesting, dynamic and exhilarating moments in all of amateur and professional sport. Both at home and abroad, nationally and internationally, Canadian athletes have always been at the forefront of the world's best, close on the heels of the top athletes and in many cases surpassing them. The number of Canadian athletes achieving firsts in the country as well as the world throughout the last 100-plus years of sport is something Canadians might not have thought much about before. The goal of *Canadian Sports Records* is to bring these athletes' accomplishments to light and celebrate the huge amount of talent Canada has had and still has swimming in its pools, boxing in its rings, pitching on its diamonds, running on its tracks, skating on its ice...

Chapter 1 focuses on Canada's record-breakers and sports phenoms in amateur sport worldwide and at the Olympics, with a special section that looks back at various Olympic Games to highlight Canada's most notable performances. The second part of *Canadian Sports Records* switches gears to professional sports, highlighting athletes such as Steve Nash, Jason Bay, Gilles Villeneuve, Mike Weir and Wayne Gretzky. Throughout both chapters, various Olympic, Canadian and world statistics have been inserted in order to show how Canadian athletes measure up when it gets down to actual facts. In many record books, the accomplishments of athletes are left simply to the numbers, but by providing both the stories and the statistics behind the records, readers of this book will hopefully obtain a sense of pride in their nation's athletes as well as enjoy their trials and triumphs on the road to sporting success. World standings are included beside Canadian ones to illustrate that while Canada doesn't always hold the world record, its athletes are often just shy of overtaking the leaders. And as is written in this book, in some cases Canadian athletes have done just that.

Chapter One

Canadians on the World Stage

SUMMER SPORTS

Swimming

Brent Hayden, Colin Russell, Rick Say and
Joel Greenshields

Generally speaking, within the world of competitive swimming, Canadians are not the biggest fish in the pool, and going into the 2008 Beijing Summer Olympics, Canada's expectations in the pool were modest. Canada had not taken a medal in an Olympic pool since Curtis Myden won a bronze in the 400-metre individual medley at the 2000 Summer Games in Sydney, Australia. However, a few promising Canadian athletes were hopefuls in Beijing's futuristic swimming cube. Mission, BC's Brent Hayden; Toronto's Colin Russell; Victoria, BC's

Rick Say; and Airdrie, Alberta's Joel Greenshields had the potential to medal in the 4x100-metre freestyle relay, but when placed up against the swimming power of nations like the United States, there was no doubt Canada had to pull off an upset to make it to the podium.

The relay team combined for several strong preliminaries to put Canada into the finals. Facing tough competition against the likes of the Americans, Australians and French, the Canadians thought if they pushed hard enough they could challenge for a medal. Hayden even gave up his spot in the 200-metre freestyle semifinal so he would be fresh for the relay that same day:

"I knew it was going to go faster than yesterday," said Hayden after the race. *"That's just the way the world's going. I think it was a really good decision and I don't think I could have gone a 47.56 if I'd done the 200 this morning. It came down to sacrificing my individual performance for the good of the team."*

At the sound of the starting bell, Hayden got the team off to a brilliant start, keeping relative pace with his competitors. Tagging up, Hayden passed the baton to Greenshields who likewise swam a great race but began to fall behind the leaders. Halfway through the race, the Canadian team was well behind the first-place American swimmers but still on pace for the world record, strangely enough. Russell took the third position while Say held the anchor leg. When the team crossed the finish line, they could hardly believe their eyes when they looked up at the times. The Canadians had just broken the previous world record but had come in sixth place. Canada's time was 3:12.46 while the gold-medalist American team set a new world record for the 4x100-metre freestyle relay with a time of 3:08.24.

Julia Wilkinson

Stratford, Ontario native Julia Wilkinson also had high hopes for the 2008 Beijing Olympics. Her specialty in the pool was the backstroke, and in competitions leading up to the Summer Games, she had proven herself as one of Canada's top medal hopefuls by setting Canadian records in the 50-metre backstroke at the 2008 Summer Nationals (28.53 seconds) and in the 100-metre backstroke at the Nationals (1:00.56). Wilkinson felt it was her time to shine and bring Canada some respect in the pool, but she was up against many other fast competitors in Beijing. With recent technological developments in swimwear, athletes were breaking records in droves at their Olympic trials, and Wilkinson knew that although she might break her own personal record in China, beating the best in the world would take some extra perseverance.

In her 100-metre backstroke semifinal, Wilkinson set a new Canadian record with a time of 1:00.38, but she could not best herself to get into the finals and finished 12th. But even though she achieved a new Canadian record and a personal best in the event, Wilkinson saw her effort as a defeat. "I should have made the final," she told a reporter after the race. "It's disappointing because I know I have that in me."

Despite her broken dreams, this was Wilkinson's first Olympics, and she will more than likely return to break more records in the future. While at Beijing she also helped her 4x100-metre relay teammates Montréal natives Audrey Lacroix and Geneviève Saumur, and Calgary's Erica Morningstar break another Canadian record with 3:38.32 in the event. Unfortunately the foursome was not fast enough to reach the podium, but Canada will be looking for Wilkinson and her teammates once again in London at the 2012 Olympics.

Record-breaking Fact

The first woman to swim across the English Channel and back was Canada's Cynthia Nichols, who completed the arduous trip in 19 hours 55 minutes on September 7–8, 1977.

Ryan Cochrane

Another Canadian hopeful in Beijing was Victoria, BC's Ryan Cochrane in the 1500-metre freestyle. Having made it through the semifinals, Cochrane was ready to participate in the gold-medal race that took place on the last day of the Olympic swimming competition. Cochrane was Canada's last hope of bringing home a swimming medal at Beijing, and things looked good— he was, after all, the Canadian record-holder in the event with a time of 14:40.84, a pace he had set earlier in the third heat.

Lining up in Lane 5 beside Cochrane in the final was Olympic record-holder and 1500-metre defending champion from the 2000 and 2004 Olympics, Australia's Grant Hackett. This positioning played out in Cochrane's favour through the entire race because he was able to keep an eye on how Hackett was swimming. The gun went off, and in the first 500 metres Cochrane led all the swimmers and had a lead of three-tenths-of-a-second over Hackett (which might not sound like much, but in swimming is at least an arm's length). But at the 1000-metre mark Hackett began to surge, and Tunisian swimmer Oussama Mellouli swam into the lead. Cochrane couldn't keep pace with them. Fending off American and Russian swimmers who were well within striking distance of Cochrane's third place, he gave a final push to touch the wall and locked up his bronze medal.

"I'm so happy with it," said Cochrane after the race. "It was a hard race and I think the first half took a lot out of me for the second half. But I just couldn't be happier." Cochrane's swimming-event Olympic medal was the first for a Canadian in eight years, and his Canadian-record time was the 26th national record set in the Beijing pool. For Cochrane, it was the perfect ending to a perfect Olympics.

Alex Baumann

Moving away from Beijing, no other Canadian has dominated the sport of swimming like Alex Baumann. During the early-to-late 1980s, Baumann owned most Canadian records in the sport and set a few world records along his path to Canadian sports glory.

Born in Prague, Baumann moved to Canada with his parents when he was six years old. While friends enrolled in hockey, at the age of nine Baumann signed up for competitive swimming and progressed quickly. By the time he was 17, Baumann had 38 Canadian swimming records to his name and a world record in the 200-metre individual medley. He continued his stellar rise to the top of the swimming world by bettering his 200-metre individual medley record at the 1982 Commonwealth Games in Brisbane, Australia, with a time of 2:02.25. He also won the gold medal in the 400-metre individual medley at those same Games.

Set for the ultimate in international glory at the 1984 Olympics in Los Angeles, Baumann suffered a tragic setback when his father died of complications from diabetes and his brother committed suicide shortly thereafter. In a show of extreme strength and courage, Baumann persevered through his personal tragedies and entered the 1984 Olympics as one of the world's favourites to walk away with one or more gold.

Baumann continued his domination of the pool by winning both the 400-metre individual medley and the 200-metre individual medley, breaking the world record in each event. He was the star of the 1984 Canadian Olympic team and received countless awards for his performance at the Games. Baumann continued to compete up until the late 1980s before retiring and using his experience to teach younger athletes the sport of swimming.

Record-breaking Fact

In 1956, Irene MacDonald won Canada's first-ever diving medal when she took home the bronze in the springboard event.

Anne Ottenbrite

When Anne Ottenbrite showed up at the Olympic pool in 1984 in Los Angeles she was unknown to the world, including most of Canada. However, the 18-year-old from Bowmanville, Ontario, surprised the world and even herself by winning three medals.

It was a miracle she had even made it this far because of her curious habit of getting into accidents. Two months before the Games, Ottenbrite dislocated her right knee while trying on a pair of high heels. Luckily she recovered in time to make it to the Olympics, but while in Los Angeles she suffered whiplash in a car accident. To top it off, she then strained a thigh muscle when she got overexcited playing a video game. Despite all her injuries and bad luck, Ottenbrite was ready to compete in her first event—the 200-metre breaststroke—about an hour after fellow Canadian Alex Baumann won his first gold medal.

Going into the race, oddsmakers and pundits predicted Ottenbrite would finish in the bronze-medal position, at best. American Susan Rapp was expected to take home the gold. Ottenbrite had a different answer for her naysayers— she completed the race in first place, almost a full second ahead of second-place finisher Rapp. In winning the race, Ottenbrite became the first Canadian female to win a gold medal in an Olympic pool.

But the spunky swimmer was not finished. Three days later she was back, winning silver in the 100-metre breaststroke and a bronze in the 4x100-metre medley relay. The Olympic Games might have started out unlucky for Ottenbrite, but she definitely finished them in style.

Victor Davis

Born in Guelph, Ontario, a young Victor Davis learned how to swim in the pristine Canadian lakes around his home. All that practice in the water paid off, and when Davis started competing, he turned heads wherever he went. Unable to go to the 1980 Olympics in Moscow because of the Canadian boycott, Davis' big international coming-out party was at the 1982 World Championships in Guayaquil, Ecuador, where he finished his 200-metre breaststroke final with a gold medal and a world record. He won a silver medal in the 100-metre breaststroke in Ecuador as well.

With an impressive resumé, Davis finally got his shot at the Olympics in 1984 in Los Angeles. Going in as the favourite in the breaststroke events, Davis had a lot of pressure on his shoulders but knew how to compete and approached the races with gold in his sights. In his first final, he ended up breaking the world record in the 100-metre breaststroke, but had to settle for a silver medal, losing out by a few tenths of a second to American swimmer Steve Lundquist. Davis, unfazed by the loss, rebounded in the 200-metre breaststroke by winning gold and establishing a new world record in the process. The new record time of 2:13.34 shaved an incredible 1.24 seconds off Davis' old record of 2:14.58.

He also swam with teammates Thomas Ponting, Michael West and Sandy Goss in the 4x100-metre medley relay and helped Canada to another silver medal. For Davis' efforts in the pool at the 1984 Olympics, he was named Swimming Canada's male athlete of the year and made a member of the Order of Canada.

During his career Davis set several world records, won 29 national titles and claimed 16 medals in international competition. He also won another Olympic silver medal in the 4x100-metre medley at the 1988 Olympics in Seoul. Davis retired from competitive swimming in 1989, and shortly afterward, he was struck by a car in a hit-and-run while leaving a bar in rural Québec and died a few days later.

Elaine Tanner

Elaine Tanner, of Vancouver, BC, burst onto the international swimming scene as a 15-year-old in 1966 at the Commonwealth Games in Kingston, Jamaica. She set two world records in the 220-metre butterfly and 440-metre individual medley, and won an astounding four gold medals and three silver medals. The first woman to ever win four gold medals at a Commonwealth Games, Tanner was subsequently named Cana 's Athlete of the Year—the youngest recipien of the award in its history. The following year, Tanner continued her medal-winning streak and took home five medals at the Pan American Games in Winnipeg. "Mighty Mouse" Tanner also broke two more world records in the 200-metre backstroke and 100-metre backstroke on her way to the podium in 1968. Tanner went on to compete in that year's Olympic Games in Mexico City, where she claimed three medals and became the first-ever Canadian to win three medals in a single Olympic Games. She retired from swimming after Mexico City, at the age of 18.

George Hodgson

One of Canada's most remarkable athletes in the first half of the 20th century, George Hodgson was this country's Michael Phelps of the day. At the 1912 Summer Olympics in Stockholm, Sweden, Hodgson walked into the Games as the odds-on favourite to win in the pool after coming off an incredible performance at the 1911 Coronation Games in London, England. Swimming in the freestyle 400-metre, 1000-metre, 1500-metre and mile distances in Stockholm, Hodgson set four world records and won two Olympic gold medals. He smashed his own world record in the 1500-metre event by an incredible two minutes and 33 seconds and bested his record in the 400-metre race as well.

Canadian Male 50m Swimming Records

Event	Time	Athlete	Year	Location
50 free	22.19	Brent Hayden	2006	Melbourne (Australia)
100 free	47.56	Brent Hayden	2008	Beijing (China)
200 free	1:46.40	Brent Hayden	2008	Beijing (China)
400 free	3:44.85	Ryan Cochrane	2008	Beijing (China)
800 free	7:47.11	Ryan Cochrane	2008	Beijing (China)
1500 free	14:40.84	Ryan Cochrane	2008	Beijing (China)
50 back	25.72	Callum Ng	2007	Bangkok (Thailand)
100 back	53.98	Mark Tewksbury	1992	Beijing (China)
200 back	1:58.50	Keith Beavers	2008	Beijing (China)
50 breast	28.22	Morgan Knabe	2003	World Championship Trials (Canada)
100 breast	1:00.70	Morgan Knabe	2003	World Championship Trials (Canada)
200 breast	2:08.84	Mike Brown	2008	Beijing (China)
50 fly	23.81	Thomas Kindler	2007	Summer Nationals (Canada)
100 fly	52.28	Joe Bartoch	2008	Beijing (China)
200 fly	1:57.45	Adam Sioui	2008	Beijing (China)
200 IM	1:59.19	Ketih Beavers	2008	Beijing (China)
400 IM	4:11.41	Brian Johns	2008	Beijing (China)
400m MR	3:34.99	Jake Tapp	2008	Tri-Nations, Québec City (Canada)
		Mathieu Bois		
		Joe Bartoch		
		Joel Greenshields		
400m FR	3:12.26	Brent Hayden	2008	Beijing (China)
		Joel Greenshields		
		Colin Russell		
		Rick Say		

Canadian Male cont.

Event	Time	Athlete	Year	Location
800m FR	7:05.77	Colin Russell	2008	Beijing (China)
		Brian Johns		
		Brent Hayden		
		Andrew Hurd		

World Male 50m Swimming Records

Event	Time	Athlete	Year	Location
50 free	21.28	Eamon Sullivan (AUS)	2008	Sydney (Australia)
100 free	47.05	Eamon Sullivan (AUS)	2008	Beijing (China)
200 free	1:42.96	Michael Phelps (USA)	2008	Beijing (China)
400 free	3:40.08	Ian Thorpe (AUS)	2002	Manchester (UK)
800 free	7:38.65	Grant Hackett (AUS)	2005	Montréal (Canada)
1500 free	14:34.56	Grant Hackett (AUS)	2001	Fukuoka (Japan)
50 back	24.33	Randall Bal (USA)	2008	Eindhoven (Netherlands)
100 back	52.54	Aaron Peirsol (USA)	2008	Beijing (China)
200 back	1:53.94	Ryan Lochte (USA)	2008	Beijing (China)
50 breast	27.18	Oleg Lisogor (UKR)	2002	Berlin (Germany)
100 breast	58.91	Kosuke Kitajima (JPN)	2008	Beijing (China)
200 breast	2:07.51	Kosuke Kitajima (JPN)	2008	Tokyo (Japan)
50 fly	22.96	Roland Schoeman (SAF)	2005	Montréal (Canada)
100 fly	50.40	Ian Crocker (USA)	2008	Montréal (Canada)
200 fly	1:52.03	Michael Phelps (USA)	2008	Beijing (China)
200 IM	1:54.23	Michael Phelps (USA)	2008	Beijing (China)
400 IM	4:03.84	Michael Phelps (USA)	2008	Beijing (China)
400m MR	3:29.34	Aaron Peirsol	2008	Beijing (China)
		Brendan Hansen		
		Michael Phelps		
		Jason Lezak (USA)		

World Male cont.

Event	Time	Athlete	Year	Location
400m FR	3:08.24	Michael Phelps	2008	Beijing (China)
		Garret Weber-Gale		
		Cullen Jones		
		Jason Lezak (USA)		
800m FR	6:58.56	Michael Phelps	2008	Beijing (China)
		Ryan Lochte		
		Ricky Berens		
		Peter Vadernkaay (USA)		

Canadian Female 50m Swimming Records

Event	Time	Athlete	Year	Location
50 free	25.47	Victoria Poon	2008	Beijing (China)
100 free	54.08	Erica Morningstar	2007	Melbourne (Australia)
200 free	1:58.00	Stephanie Horner	2008	Beijing (China)
400 free	4:07.32	Brittany Reimer	2005	Montréal (Canada)
800 free	8:27.59	Brittany Reimer	2005	Montréal (Canada)
1500 free	16:07.73	Brittany Reimer	2005	Montréal (Canada)
50 back	28.53	Julia Wilkinson	2008	Summer Nationals (Canada)
100 back	1:00.38	Julia Wilkinson	2008	Beijing (China)
200 back	2:11.16	Jennifer Fratesi	2001	Fukuoka (Japan)
50 breast	31.25	Amanda Reason	2008	Monterrey (Mexico)
100 breast	1:07.78	Annamay Pierse	2007	Rio (Brazil)
200 breast	2:23.77	Annamay Pierse	2008	Beijing (China)
50 fly	27.17	Shona Kitson	2000	Summer Nationals (Canada)
100 fly	58.88	Mackenzie Downing	2007	Bangkok (Thailand)
200 fly	2:06.83	Audrey Lacroix	2007	Bangkok (Thailand)

Canadian Female cont.

Event	Time	Athlete	Year	Location
200 IM	2:12.03	Julia Wilkinson	2008	Beijing (China)
400 IM	4:38.46	Joanne Malar	1999	Winnipeg (Canada)
4x100m MR	4:01.35	Julia Wilkinson	2008	Beijing (China)
		Annamay Pierse		
		Audrey Lacroix		
		Erica Morningstar		
4x100m FR	3:38.32	Julia Wilkinson	2008	Beijing (China)
		Erica Morningstar		
		Audrey Lacroix		
		Genevieve Saumur		
4x200m FR	7:56.26	Stephanie Horner	2008	Beijing (China)
		Erica Morningstar		
		Genevieve Samur		
		Julia Wilkinson		

World Female 50m Swimming Records

Event	Time	Athlete	Year	Location
50 free	23.97	Lisbeth Trickett (AUS)	2008	Sydney (Australia)
100 free	52.88	Lisbeth Trickett (AUS)	2008	Sydney (Australia)
200 free	1:54.82	Federica Pellegrini (ITA)	2008	Beijing (China)
400 free	4:01.53	Federica Pellegrini (ITA)	2008	Eindhoven (Netherlands)
800 free	8:14.10	Rebecca Adlington (GBR)	2008	Beijing (China)
1500 free	15:42.54	Kate Ziegler (USA)	2007	Mission Viejo (U.S.)
50 back	27.67	Sophie Edington (AUS)	2008	Sydney (Australia)
100 back	58.77	Kristy Coventry (SAF)	2008	Beijing (China)
200 back	2:05.24	Kristy Coventry (SAF)	2008	Beijing (China)

World Female cont.

Event	Time	Athlete	Year	Location
50 breast	30.31	Jade Edmistone (AUS)	2006	Melbourne (Australia)
100 breast	1:05.09	Leisel Jones (AUS)	2006	Melbourne (Australia)
200 breast	2:20.22	Rebecca Soni (USA)	2008	Beijing (China)
50 fly	25.46	Theresa Alshammar (SWE)	2007	Barcelona (Spain)
100 fly	56.61	Inge de Bruijn (NED)	2000	Sydney Olympics (Australia)
200 fly	2:04.18	Liu Zige (CHN)	2008	Beijing (China)
200 IM	2:08.45	Stephanie Rice (AUS)	2008	Beijing (China)
400 IM	4:29.45	Stephanie Rice (AUS)	2008	Beijing (China)
4x100m MR	3:52.69	Emily Seebohm	2008	Beijing (China)
		Leisel Jones		
		Jessicah Schipper		
		Lisbeth Trickett (AUS)		
4x100m FR	3:33.62	Inge Dekker	2008	Eindhoven (Netherlands)
		Ranomi Kromowidjojo		
		Femke Heemskerk		
		Marleen Veldhuis (NED)		
4x200m FR	7:44.31	Stephanie Rice	2008	Beijing (China)
		Bronte Barratt		
		Kylie Palmer		
		Linda Mackenzie (AUS)		

Rowing

Kathleen Heddle and Marnie McBean

When it comes to Olympic gold medals, Kathleen Heddle and Marnie McBean are no strangers to glory. Competing together in various rowing events for many years to eventually become the first Canadians to win three Summer Olympic gold medals, each rower of this duo had different beginnings in the sport.

Heddle, born in Trail, BC, didn't touch an oar until she was 19 years old and attending the University of British Columbia. She picked up a paddle after her high hopes of making the varsity volleyball team were dashed, and the university's rowing coach spotted her at class registration, thinking she would be a good fit for the crew. Just two years after joining the varsity rowing team, Heddle became part of the national team and won a gold medal in the straight pairs event at the 1987 Pan American Games. Heddle continued to row with great success, meeting future Olympic teammate McBean along the way.

McBean, born in Vancouver, BC, began rowing in 1985 after attending a learn-to-row course at the Toronto Argonaut Club. Only one year later she captured a bronze medal at the 1986 World Junior Championships. She never looked back, later joining the national team and competing with Heddle. The pair was unstoppable and proved their dominance over the world of women's rowing as double world champions in the coxless pairs and women's eight events in 1991. Heddle counts the pair's win in 1991 as her most memorable. "My favourite race is the 1991 World Championship pair because that's the first major race that we won. That was our breakthrough."

Heddle and McBean went on to take gold at the 1992 Barcelona Olympics in coxless pairs and eights. In the final of the eights events, McBean said afterwards the push to the win took everything she had:

> It felt as if we were moments away from having nothing left. The crowd was going crazy and I'm thinking, "Where's the finish line?" It was just great to have it done. That was the first thing that went through my head.

Heddle decided to retire from rowing after Barcelona, but was lured back into the sport by McBean and convinced to go for one more gold at the 1996 Atlanta Olympics in a switch to sculling boats. It turned out to be a good choice, as in preparation for Atlanta, Heddle won a silver medal with McBean in double sculls at the 1994 World Championships, followed by a gold in the double sculls and silver in the quadruple sculls in

1995 at the same event. Prepared for Atlanta, Heddle and McBean found success once again, taking gold in the double sculls and bronze in quadruple sculls. Despite having won gold before, McBean said she was still speechless immediately after the Atlanta win. "I couldn't catch my breath, let alone say anything," she said at the time.

Heddle retired for good after Atlanta but has never been forgotten as one of two of Canada's most decorated female Summer Olympians (the other is McBean). In 1997, Heddle was given the Order of British Columbia and inducted into the Canadian Sports Hall of Fame. She was also awarded rowing's highest honour, the Thomas Keller Medal, in 1999 by the International Rowing Federation for her outstanding career in international rowing. She has no regrets about her decision to walk away from rowing after 1996, saying:

I miss rowing in the sense that there's nothing like it and there will never be anything like it for me again, but not in the sense that I still wish I could be out there competing. I had a great career and I stopped at exactly the right time.

Largely stepping away from the limelight in her post-Olympic life, Heddle remains the opposite of McBean.

McBean, on the other hand, went on after 1996 with expectations of competing in the 2000

Sydney Olympics. She had to withdraw due to a back injury, but stayed on to support her Canadian teammates competing in Sydney. At the end of her career, McBean had 23 World Cup victories, 12 career Olympic and World Championship medals and was the first woman to claim a medal in every boat class at World and Olympic events. Bouncing back from her 2000 back injury, McBean competed in her first Olympic-distance triathlon in 2001, climbed Mount Kilimanjaro in 2002 and as recently as 2009 is an athlete mentor with the Canadian Olympic Committee.

Record-breaking Fact

The first sailor to complete a solo circumnavigation of the world was Canadian Joshua Slocum. Abroad his 36-foot boat Spray, Slocum began his journey in Boston, Massachusetts, in April 1895 and ended it three years, two months and two days later in Newport, Rhode Island. In total, he sailed just over 74,000 kilometres.

Kayaking
Adam van Koeverden

Naming Adam van Koeverden as Canada's flag-bearer for the 2008 Beijing Olympic opening ceremonies wasn't a difficult choice. The reigning world and Olympic champion in the K-1 500-metre individual kayaking race, this Oakville, Ontario native first burst onto the scene in 1999 when he won a bronze medal in the K-1 1000-metre event at the World Junior Championships in Zagreb, Croatia. Working up to the 2004 Athens Olympics with a silver already claimed at the 2003 World Championships, van Koeverden took the gold medal in the K-1 500-metre race and a bronze in the 1000-metre event. For his efforts he was chosen as the Canadian flag-bearer at the Athens closing ceremonies and named the 2004 Lou Marsh Trophy recipient as Canadian athlete of the year. Although van Koeverden accepted the award graciously, in a CBC interview he admitted that aside from kayaking, he was never really much of an athlete:

> *I would be lying if I said I was. I have some abilities as an athlete, clearly. I have very good pain tolerance and my endurance is good. I'm a good runner. But I can't really dribble a basketball or kick a soccer ball. And I sink in the pool.*

Winning a host of other medals at competitions around the world after Athens, van Koeverden trained hard for Beijing. At the World Cup competition in Pozna, Poland, in June 2008, he let the world know he was the best in his sport when he set a new Canadian and world record in the K-1 500-metre race with a time of 1:35.630. His appointment as Canadian flag-bearer at the opening ceremonies in Beijing was a natural choice.

In 2004 when I entered the stadium, I tripped, so I think the main thing I'll be thinking about is left-right, left-right to keep my feet up and not falling. I'm not worried about being emotional about carrying the flag, I've done it before in Athens at the closing ceremonies so I know what to expect, and I can't see any negative aspect to carrying the flag at the opening ceremonies.

While the ceremonies went by without a problem, van Koeverden stumbled in the K-1 1000-metre final, finishing well out of third. But he did manage to take home a silver medal in the K-1 500-metre race, where he broke his own world-record time. Still in his twenties while at Beijing, it is assured that van Koeverden will return to the 2012 London Olympics, and Canada will have the chance to cheer for him once again.

Running

Donovan Bailey

At the Olympics, the 100-metre sprint is the marquee event. Over the years a certain mystique has grown in Canada and around the world in the battle to become of the world's fastest man. Canadians remember Ben Johnson's defeat of long-time rival American Carl Lewis at the 1988 Games in Seoul in world-record time—and then the performance-enhancing drug scandal that saw Johnson stripped of his medal. Before Johnson, the last Canadian to hold the title of fastest man in the world was Percy Williams when he won the gold at the 1928 Olympics in Amsterdam.

Donovan Bailey first made a name for himself at the 1995 World Championships in Gothenburg, Sweden, when he won the gold medal in the 100-metre sprint and helped the Canadian squad take the top spot in the 4x100-metre relay. The new Canadian dominance in these events was a significant change from years of American rule. From Carl Lewis to Maurice Greene, the U.S. had long lorded over track's high-profile sprinting events. Bailey was out to challenge that dominance and stepped up at the 1996 Olympic Games in Atlanta to do so.

The anticipation in Atlanta's Olympic stadium was high as the athletes took their positions on the 100-metre sprint starting line—and it mounted as defending British Olympic champion Linford Christie false-started and was then followed by Trinidad's Ato Boldon. Christie false-started again, and when the track official gestured for Christie to leave the track because two false starts equals a disqualification, the Briton refused to leave. Christie's angry gestures did not sway officials, and he was forced out of the race.

Finally, on the fourth try, the race got off to a clean start. Bailey began characteristically slow but at the 50-metre point turned on the speed and surged ahead of the competition. At the finish line he was a full stride ahead of second-place finisher Namibia's Frankie Fredericks. Not only had Bailey won Canada the gold in the 100-metre event, but he had also broken the world and Olympic record with a time of 9.84 seconds. And that Olympic record would stand until 2008 in Beijing when Jamaican Usain Bolt ran the 100-metre sprint in a time of 9.69 seconds.

Record-breaking Fact

The first runner to win two consecutive Boston marathons was a Canadian; John Caffery took the top spot in 1900 and 1901. Canadian Gerard Cote also won the Boston Marathon—four times—in his running career: in 1940, 1943, 1944 and 1948. He completed the 1940 marathon faster than anyone had before in an impressive time of 2:28:28.

Percy Williams

When Vancouver, BC native Percy Williams tried out at the Canadian Olympic trials in 1928, he surprised many people—including himself—when he won both the 100-metre and 200-metre sprint events. Without any previous major competitive history, Williams was put onto a ship and sent to Amsterdam to compete with the rest of Team Canada in the 1928 Olympics. Of the semifinals for the 100-metre sprint, Williams later mused in his journal at how easily he managed to make it through to the finals. "My ideals of the Olympic Games are all shot. I always imagined it was a game of heroes. Well, I'm in the semifinals myself so it can't be so hot."

During the final, the 126-pound Williams was dwarfed by some of the other competitors, the largest of whom was the six-foot, 200-pound Jack London from Great Britain. At the sound of the gun, Williams got off to an incredible start and created enough distance between himself and his competitors to finish in first and take the gold medal in 10.8 seconds. Williams continued his blasé attitude in his journal entry after the race. "Well, well, well. So I'm supposed to be the World's 100m Champion. No more fun in running now."

Two days later the gold medalist was back on the track to take part in the 200-metre sprint. In

22 seconds he had himself another gold medal, beating out favourite Helmut Körnig from Germany. But Williams wasn't yet finished with racing. He won the 100-yard dash at the inaugural 1930 British Empire Games (later renamed the Commonwealth Games) and set the world record in 10.3 seconds in the 100-metre sprint that same year. An injury to his thigh muscle sidelined Williams shortly afterward, and he never fully recovered. He tried a comeback at the 1932 Olympics in Los Angeles but failed to make the finals. Upon returning to Canada he hung up his running shoes for good and became an insurance agent. Alone after his mother died in 1977 and living in constant pain from arthritis, Williams took his own life in 1982.

Record-breaking Fact

Phil Edwards, a competitor in the 4x400-metre relay, 800-metre and 1500-metre track events and Canada's "Man of Bronze," earned his then Canadian record with a fifth career Olympic bronze medal while participating at the 1936 Games in Berlin, Germany.

Hurdles
Perdita Felicien

When Perdita Felicien was making her way through the ranks of amateur hurdling, Canada could tell she was destined for great things. She possessed excellent speed and amazing technical know-how. It was only a matter of time before Felicien, from Oshawa, Ontario, made a name for herself on the international scene.

After an exemplary start to her career at the university level, Felicien moved up to bigger things in 2003 when she won the gold medal at the World Championships of Athletics in Paris, France, beating out some of her toughest competitors. She was Canada's rising track star, and an entire nation was watching her every move.

Felicien further notched up the attention when in 2004 at a track meet in Eugene, Oregon, she set a new Canadian record in the 100-metre hurdles by running a world-class time of 12.46 seconds. This new Canadian record placed her at the top of the ladder among Canadian athletes and moved her alongside hurdler greats such as Americans Gail Devers and Michelle Perry. Felicien racked up win after win leading up to the 2004 Summer Olympics in Athens, Greece, and was hands-down the gold-medal favourite. All she needed to do was win in Athens to live up to her reputation, and for Canadian fans, hers was one of the most anticipated finals in track and field since Donovan Bailey captured the gold in the 100-metre sprint in world-record time at the 1996 Atlanta Olympics. On August 24, 2004, every Canadian camera was focused on Felicien as she took her position.

Felicien burst out of the blocks, but something went wrong at the first hurdle. As she lifted her lead leg to jump, she caught the edge of the hurdle and fell. Landing awkwardly, she stumbled into the lane of Russian runner Irina Shevchenko and knocked her out of the race as well. Grimacing in pain, Felicien stared down the track as someone other than her ran to Olympic glory.

Immediately after the race, the CBC interviewed a distraught Felicien who apologized to Canada. She made her return to competitive hurdles after the 2004 Olympic upset, winning silver at the 2007 World Championships, and Canadians look forward to what's next for Felicien.

Record-breaking Fact

A relative unknown, George Orton of Strathroy, Ontario, won the gold medal in the 2500-metre steeplechase at the 1900 Olympics in Paris,

France, as well as the bronze in the 400-metre hurdles. He took home the only medals Canada won at the 1900 Olympics, but it wasn't until years later that Canada realized he had actually won under the maple leaf. Orton attended college in the U.S. and excelled on the track team, but when it came time to go to the Olympics, it was clear Canada was not going to pay his way so he hitched a ride with his American compatriots. His victories were celebrated under the U.S. flag at the time but are now honoured in Canada after his heritage was discovered by historians.

Earl Thomson

Born near the town of Prince Albert, Saskatchewan, Earl Thomson moved to California when he was eight years old. Growing up and training in the United States, Thomson retained his Canadian citizenship, and just before the 1920 Olympic Games in Antwerp, Belgium, was considered one of the best hurdlers in the world. America hoped he would race under its flag, but Thomson's roots ran deep in Canadian soil, and he chose to run for Canada instead.

Thomson easily won the gold medal in the 110-metre hurdles in an Olympic- and world-record time of 14.8 seconds. That year he also broke the world record in the 120-yard hurdles, which he finished in a time of 14.4 seconds.

Heptathlon
Jessica Zelinka

Not long before the 2008 Beijing Olympics, 26-year-old heptathlete Jessica Zelinka of London, Ontario, was unsure if she would make the trip to China given that the previous summer she had suffered a plantar fascia tear in her right foot and was taken out of competition. The injury prevented her from attending the pre-Olympic World Championships and put a dent in her training routine. Pushing hard, Zelinka returned to form in time for Beijing as Canada's only representative in the gruelling two-day heptathlon event.

The first day of the event began with the 100-metre hurdles—an event she had never finished in less than 13 seconds. It was a fast field, but at the sound of the gun, Zelinka leapt out of the blocks and bounded over the first hurdle with a slight edge on the pack. She hit the finish line in second place with a time of 12.97 seconds, a personal best. The finish gave her 1129 points.

Zelinka put in a valiant effort in her next event, high jump, but could not break the

1.77-metre mark, two centimetres off her personal best. The event gave her another 941 points.

In shot put, Zelinka consistently recorded shorter-than-normal throws for her skill level. Her farthest shot landed at 13.79 metres, a full metre-and-a-half off her personal best. Zelinka's shot put score gave her another 780 points.

The last event on the first day of competition was the 200-metre sprint, and the Canadian was looking to move up in the standings after her poor showing in the shot put event. She ended up with a personal best in the 200-metre event (23.64 seconds), which was good for 1016 points and a grand total of 3866 points on the day.

On day two of the heptathlon, Zelinka started off in the long jump. She hit 6.12 metres taking off from her left foot—the opposite foot she was used to—due to her injury. "Happy to do that with my first jump. A personal best for my left foot," said Zelinka afterward. The long jump added another 887 points to her event total. Next was the javelin, which gave her another 742 points.

The final event of the heptathlon was the 800-metre race. Zelinka was sixth place overall, and a strong finish in the 800-metre event could move her up one or two spots in the standings. Using what little energy she had left, Zelinka ended her Olympic experience with a personal best of 2:07.99 in the 800-metre, good for 995 points. Her points total of 6490 in the heptathlon was a new Canadian record. "I came here, got a Canadian record, was close to what I was aiming for and finished strong," said Zelinka to the *Montreal Gazette* after her final event.

Zelinka will return to training in preparation for the 2012 Games in London in which she has aspirations of becoming one of the top-three heptathletes in the world.

High Jump
Duncan McNaughton

Duncan McNaughton of Cornwall, Ontario, won Canada's first and only men's Olympic gold medal in the high jump at the 1932 Olympics in Los Angeles. He almost wasn't allowed to compete in the Games because he was disqualified at the 1930 British Empire Games for diving over the high bar, but officials reversed their decision and McNaughton took home the gold with a jump of 1.97 metres.

Ethel Catherwood

Saskatoon's Ethel Catherwood was the world's first woman to win a gold medal in the Olympic high jump. She won the event at the 1928 Olympics in Amsterdam with jump of 1.59 metres, and is the only Canadian female to take home an individual Olympic gold in a track-and-field event.

Shot Put
Dylan Armstrong

Kamloops, BC native Dylan Armstrong would have liked nothing better than to walk away from his first Olympic experience in Beijing in 2008 with a medal around his neck, but it just wasn't meant to be. Going into the Games, Armstrong was Canada's best hope for a medal in the shot put event, with a new Canadian record already established earlier in the year. He was up against some tough competition, but the three-and-a-half years he spent in preparation for this Olympic moment gave him the confidence he needed to make a push for the podium.

Armstrong put together a series of powerful tosses that put him in a good position for a medal. On his final throw he threw the 7.26-kilogram ball to a new Canadian-record distance of 21.04 metres, far enough to place him in the bronze-medal position with just one shot-putter left capable of besting his distance: American Christian Cantwell. Unfortunately, Cantwell delivered a 21.09-metre toss that catapulted him into second place, moving Armstrong down to fourth position. Tomasz Majewski of Poland took home the gold medal (21.51 metres), Cantwell the silver and the bronze went to Belarusian Andrei Mikhnevich (21.05 metres). Armstrong missed out on his first Olympic medal by one centimetre. Despite the lack of a medal around his neck, Armstrong gained new ground for Canadians in the shot put by not only breaking his own record but also by posting the highest-ever finish for a Canadian in shot put at the Olympics. The previously top-ranked Canadian shot-putter in the Olympics was Bishop Dolegiewicz, who placed 11th in the event at the 1984 Olympics in Los Angeles.

With the knowledge that he can compete with the best in the world, Armstrong is counting down the days until the 2012 Summer Olympics in London.

Hammer Throw

Jim Steacy

Canadian record-holder in the hammer throw, Jim Steacy went to the Olympics in Beijing in 2008 with fairly modest Canadian expectations behind him. A few months before the Games, Steacy had set the Canadian hammer-throw record at 79.13 metres and going into Beijing was therefore Canada's best hope for a top-10 finish in the event.

The 24-year-old Steacy, who was a student in kinesiology and psychology at the University of Lethbridge in Alberta, was the youngest and least experienced of the hammer throw field, having only first picked up a hammer at the age of 15. Some of the athletes competing in the event had been participating in the sport for double or triple the amount of time Steacy had. However, in the years Steacy had been swinging the hammer, he quickly climbed the ladder of international strongmen. His presence at the Olympics was, in a way, triumph enough for Steacy since the last Canadian to even qualify for the event was James Murdoch who finished in eighth place at the 1924 Olympics in Paris. But Steacy craved more: he wanted to let the world know he had arrived on the world hammer throw stage.

Stepping into the circle and gripping the handle of the hammer, Steacy shook off the nerves and put together an impressive series of throws during competition. His best toss of the event landed at 75.72 metres, just a few metres off his Canadian record. Unfortunately the distance was not enough to get Steacy into the finals, but he did move up in the world rankings to sit as the 12th-best hammer throw athlete in the world. Steacy told the *Montréal Gazette* after his final throw:

> *This is my Super Bowl, something I've worked the last nine years toward. Finally I'm here, I made the top 12 and I was competitive. Just being in it and being able to butt heads with these guys at this point in my career is all I could ask for.*

Breaking the 80-metre barrier is Steacy's next challenge, and no doubt he will do his best to make it back to the Olympics in London in 2012 to represent Canada in the hammer throw, moving himself up the world standings and closer to the podium.

Record-breaking Fact

Canada's Jim Steacy holds the national hammer throw record with a distance of 79.13 metres. The gold-medal winner at the

Beijing Olympics beat out Steacy and the others in the field by throwing the 16-pound hammer 82.02 metres. The world-record hammer toss stands at an incredible 86.74 metres, set by Yuriy Sedykh of the Soviet Union in 1986. It is expected no one will soon match the record set by Sedykh since at that time of his record-breaking throw, the sport was overrun with steroid use. The difference between top athletes then and now could measure up to 10 metres.

Canadian Records for Men's Outdoor Track and Field

Event	Time/ Distance	Athlete	Date (dd/ mm/yyyy)	Location
100m	9.84	Donovan Bailey	27/07/1996	Atlanta (U.S)
	9.84	Bruny Surin	22/08/1999	Seville (Spain)
200m	20.17	Atlee Mahorn	26/08/2001	Tokyo (Japan)
400m	44.44	Tyler Christopher	12/08/2005	Helsinki (Finland)
800m	1:43.93	Gary Reed	27/08/2006	Rieti (Italy)
1500m	3:31.71	Kevin Sullivan	30/06/2000	Rome (Italy)
Mile	3:50.26	Kevin Sullivan	28/07/2000	Oslo (Norway)
2000m	5:03.57	Steve Agar	03/06/1997	Prague (Czech Republic)
3000m	7:43.42	Jeff Schiebler	28/08/1998	Bruxelles (Belgium)
5000m	13:13.96	Jeff Schiebler	01/09/1998	Berlin (Germany)
10,000m	27:36.01	Jeff Schiebler	04/05/2001	Stanford (Canada)
Marathon	2:10:09	Jerome Drayton	07/12/1975	Fukoka (Japan)
10,000m Race Walk	39:26.02	Guillaume Leblanc	29/06/1990	Gateshead (UK)

Canadian Men Outdoor cont.

Event	Time/ Distance	Athlete	Date (dd/ mm/yyyy)	Location
20km Race Walk	1:21:03	Alberto Huerta	07/07/2000	Toronto (Canada)
30km Race Walk	2:04:56	Guillaume Leblanc	16/06/1990	Sept-Îles (Canada)
50km Race Walk	3:47:48	Marcel Jobin	20/06/1981	Terrebonne (Canada)
110m Hurdles	13.08	Mark McKoy	01/07/1993	Lille (France)
400m Hurdles	48.24	Adam Kunkel	27/07/2007	Rio de Janeiro (Brazil)
3000m Steeple-chase	8:12.58	Graeme Fell	28/08/1985	Koblenz (Germany)
4x100m Relay	3:07.77	Robert Esmie	03/08/1996	Atlanta (U.S.)
		Glenroy Gilbert		
		Bruny Surin		
		Donovan Bailey		
4x200m Relay	1:22.15	Tyler Christopher	24/04/2004	Philadelphia (U.S.)
		Shane Niemi		
		Anson Henry		
		Pierre Browne		
4x400m Relay	3:02.64	Ian Seale	31/07/1976	Montréal (Canada)
		Don Donmansky		
		Leighton Hope		
		Bryan Saunders		

Canadian Men Outdoor cont.

Event	Time/ Distance	Athlete	Date (dd/ mm/yyyy)	Location
4x800m Relay		Andrew Heaney	21/07/2007	Toronto (Canada)
		Matt Lincoln		
		Andrew Maloney		
		Kyle Smith		
4x1500m Relay	15:25.38	Greg Hutchinson	22/06/2006	London (Canada)
		Eric Gillis		
		Reid Coolsaet		
		Tylor Milne		
High Jump	2.35m	Mark Boswell	12/07/2002	Rome (Italy)
Pole Vault	5.61m	Douglas Wood	14/07/1991	Papendal (Netherlands)
Long Jump	8.20m	Edrick Floreal	20/07/1991	Sherbrooke (Canada)
Triple Jump	17.29m	Edrick Floreal	03/06/1989	Provo (U.S.)
Shot Put (7.26kg)	20.86m	Brad Snyder	18/06/2004	Atlanta (U.S.)
Discus Throw (2kg)	67.88m	Jason Tunks	14/05/1998	Abilene (U.S.)
Hammer Throw (7.26kg)	77.38m	Jim Steacy	16/07/2007	Calgary (Canada)
Javelin Throw	84.41m	Scott Russell	20/07/2005	Ottawa (Canada)
Decathlon	8626 points	Michael Smith	25–26/05/1996	Gotzis (Austria)

World Records for Men's Outdoor Track and Field

Event	Time/ Distance	Athlete	Date (dd/ mm/yyyy)	Location
100m	9.69	Usain Bolt (JAM)	16/08/2008	Beijing (China)
200m	19.30	Usain Bolt (JAM)	20/09/2008	Beijing (China)
400m	43.18	Michael Johnson (USA)	26/08/1999	Seville (Spain)
800m	1:41.11	Wilson Kipketer (DEN)	24/08/1997	Cologne (Germany)
1000m	2:11.96	Noah Ngeny (KEN)	05/09/1999	Rieti (Italy)
1500m	3:26.00	Hicham El Guerrouj (MOR)	14/07/1998	Rome (Italy)
Mile	3:43.13	Hicham El Guerrouj (MOR)	07/07/1999	Rome (Italy)
2000m	4:44.79	Hicham El Guerrouj (MOR)	07/09/1999	Berlin (Germany)
3000m	7:20.67	Daniel Komen (KEN)	01/09/1996	Rieti (Italy)
5000m	12:37.35	Kenenisa Bekele (ETH)	31/05/2004	Hengelo (Netherlands)
10,000m	26:17.53	Kenenisa Bekele (ETH)	26/08/2005	Brussels (Belgium)
Marathon	2:04:26	Haile Gebrselassie (ETH)	30/09/2007	Berlin (Germany)
10,000m Race Walk	37:53.09	Francisco J. Fernandez (ESP)	27/07/2008	Santa Cruz de Tenerife (Spain)
20km Race Walk	1:17:25.6	Bermardo Segura (MEX)	07/05/1994	Bergen (Norway)
30km Race Walk	2:01:44.1	Maurizio Damilano (ITA)	03/10/1992	Cuneo (Italy)
50km Race Walk	3:40:57.9	Thierry Toutain (FRA)	29/09/1996	Hericourt (France)

World Men Outdoor cont.

Event	Time/ Distance	Athlete	Date (dd/ mm/yyyy)	Location
110m Hurdles	12.87	Dayron Robles (CUB)	12/06/2008	Ostrava (Czech Republic)
400m Hurdles	46.78	Kevin Young (USA)	06/08/1992	Barcelona (Spain)
3000m Steeple- chase	7:53.63	Said Saaeed Shaheen (QAT)	03/09/2004	Brussels (Belgium)
4x100m Relay	37.10	Nesta Carter	22/08/2008	Beijing (China)
		Michael Frater		
		Usain Bolt		
		Asafa Powell (JAM)		
4x200m Relay	1:18.68	Michael Marsh	17/04/1994	Walnut (U.S.)
		Leroy Burrell		
		Floyd Heard		
		Carl Lewis (USA)		
4x400 m Relay	2:54.20	Jerome Young	22/07/1998	New York City (U.S.)
		Antonio Pettigrew		
		Tyree Washington		
		Michael Johnson (USA)		
4x800m Relay	7:02.43	Joseph Mutua	25/08/2006	Brussels (Belgium)
		William Yiampoy		
		Ismael Kombich		
		Wilfred Bungei (KEN)		

World Men Outdoor cont.

Event	Time/ Distance	Athlete	Date (dd/ mm/yyyy)	Location
4x1500m Relay	14:38.8	Thomas Wessinghage	17/08/1977	Cologne (Germany)
		Harald Hudak		
		Michael Lederer		
		Karl Fleschen (WGER)		
High Jump	2.45m	Javier Sotomayor (CUB)	27/07/1993	Salamanca (Spain)
Pole Vault	6.14m	Sergey Bubka (UKR)	31/07/1994	Sestriere (Italy)
Long Jump	8.95m	Mike Powell (USA)	30/08/1991	Tokyo (Japan)
Triple Jump	18.29m	Jonathan Edwards (GBR)	07/08/1995	Goteborg (Sweden)
Shot Put (7.26kg)	23.12m	Randy Barnes (USA)	20/05/1990	Westwood (U.S.)
Discus Throw (2kg)	74.08m	Jurgen Schult (EGER)	06/06/1986	Neubrandenburg (Germany)
Hammer Throw (7.26kg)	86.74m	Yuriy Sedykh (USSR)	30/08/1986	Stuttgart (Germany)
Javelin Throw	98.48m	Jan Zelezny (CZE)	25/05/1996	Jena (Germany)
Decathlon	9026 points	Roman Sebrle (CZE)	27/05/2001	Gotzis (Austria)

Canadian Records for Men's Indoor Track and Field

Event	Time/Distance	Athlete	Date (dd/mm/yyyy)	Location
50m	5.56	Donovan Bailey	09/02/1996	Reno (U.S.)
60m	6.45	Bruny Surin	13/02/1993	Leivin (France)
200m	20.66	Bruny Surin	14/02/1998	Sherbrooke (Canada)
300m	32.75	Tyler Christopher	04/02/2006	Winnipeg (Canada)
400m	46.73	Mark Jackson	11/03/1994	Indianapolis (U.S.)
600m	1:16.10	Byron Goodwin	11/03/1995	Winnipeg (Canada)
800m	1:46.47	Gary Reed	14/02/2004	Fayetteville (U.S.)
1000m	2:19.04	Simon Hoogewerf	10/02/1989	East Rutherford (U.S.)
1500m	3:38.73	Doug Consiglio	01/03/1986	Fayetteville (U.S.)
Mile	3:55.11	Nathan Brannen	29/01/2005	Boston (U.S.)
3000m	7:40.17	Kevin Sullivan	09/02/2007	Fayetteville (U.S.)
5000m	13:25.87	Jason Bunston	20/02/1997	Stockholm (Sweden)
50m Hurdles	6.25	Mark McKoy	05/03/1986	Kobe (Japan)
60m Hurdles	7.41	Mark McKoy	13/03/1993	Toronto (Canada)
5000m Race Walk	18:47.56	Tim Berrett	21/02/1993	Winnipeg (Canada)
4x200m Relay	1:24.85	Tyler Christopher	27/01/2007	Montréal (Canada)
		Adam Kunkel		
		Keston Nelson		
		Neal Hurtubise		

Canadian Men Indoor cont.

Event	Time/ Distance	Athlete	Date (dd/ mm/yyyy)	Location
4x400m Relay	3:07.77	O'Brien Gibbons	13/03/1993	Toronto (Canada)
		Mark Graham		
		Dave Anderson		
		Byron Goodwin		
4x800m Relay	7:24.50	Mike Housley	04/03/1979	Toronto (Canada)
		Paul Craig		
		Glen Bogue		
		John Craig		
High Jump	2.33m	Mark Boswell	24/02/2002	Lievin (France)
Pole Vault	5.65m	Doug Wood	15/03/1992	Winnipeg (Canada)
Long Jump	7.98m	Edrick Floreal	10/03/1989	Indianpolis (U.S.)
Triple Jump	17.14m	Edrick Floreal	11/03/1989	Indianapolis (U.S.)
Shot Put	20.32m	Brad Snyder	28/02/1998	Baton Rouge (U.S.)
Weight Throw (35 lbs.)	24.72m	Scott Russell	08/02/2002	Ames (U.S.)
Heptathlon	6279 points	Michael Smith	13–14/03/1993	Toronto (Canada)

World Records for Men's Indoor Track and Field

Event	Time/ Distance	Athlete	Date (dd/ mm/yyyy)	Location
50m	5.56	Donovan Bailey (CAN)	09/02/1996	Reno (U.S.)
60m	6.39	Maurice Greene (USA)	03/03/2001	Atlanta (U.S.)

World Men Indoor cont.

Event	Time/ Distance	Athlete	Date (dd/ mm/yyyy)	Location
200m	19.92	Frankie Fredericks (Namibia)	18/02/1996	Lievin (France)
300m	31.88	Wallace Spearmon (USA)	09/02/2005	Fayetteville (U.S.)
400m	44.57	Kerron Clement (USA)	12/03/2005	Fayetteville (U.S.)
600m	1:15.12	Nico Motchebon (GER)	28/02/1999	Sindelfingen (Germany)
800m	1:42.67	Wilson Kipketer (DEN)	09/03/1997	Paris (France)
1000m	2:14.96	Wilson Kipketer (DEN)	20/02/2000	Birmingham (England)
1500m	3:31.18	Hicham El Guerrouj (MOR)	02/02/2002	Stuttgart (Germany)
Mile	3:48.45	Hicham El Guerrouj (MOR)	12/02/1997	Ghent (Belgium)
3000m	7:24.90	Daniel Komen (KEN)	06/02/1998	Budapest (Hungary)
5000m	12:49.60	Kenenisa Bekele (ETH)	20/02/2004	Birmingham (England)
50m Hurdle	6.25	Mark McKoy (CAN)	05/86/2003	Kobe (Japan)
60m Hurdle	7.30	Colin Jackson (GBR)	06/03/1994	Sindelfingen (Germany)
5000m Race Walk	18:07.08	Mikhail Shchennikov (RUS)	14/02/1995	Moscow (Russia)
4x200m Relay	1:22.11	Linford Christie	03/03/1991	Glasgow (Scotland)
		Darren Braithwaite		
		Ade Mafe		
		John Regis (GBR)		

World Men Indoor cont.

Event	Time/ Distance	Athlete	Date (dd/ mm/yyyy)	Location
4x400m Relay	3:02.83	Andre Morris	07/03/1999	Maebashi (Japan)
		Dameon Johnson		
		Deon Minor		
		Milton Campbell (USA)		
4x800m Relay	7:13.94	Joey Woody	06/02/2000	Roxbury Crossing (U.S.)
		Karl Paranya		
		Rich Kenah		
		David Krummenacker (USA)		
High Jump	2.43m	Javier Sotomayor (CUB)	04/03/1989	Budapest (Hungary)
Pole Vault	6.15m	Sergey Bubka (RUS)	21/02/1993	Donets'k (Ukraine)
Long Jump	8.79m	Carl Lewis (USA)	27/01/1984	New York City (U.S.)
Triple Jump	17.83m	Christian Olsson (SWE)	07/03/2004	Budapest (Hungary)
Shot Put	22.66m	Randy Barnes (USA)	20/01/1989	Los Angeles (U.S.)
Weight Throw (35 lbs.)	25.86m	Lance Deal (USA)	04/03/1995	Atlanta (U.S.)
Heptathlon	6476 points	Dan O'Brien (USA)	13/03/1993	Toronto (Canada)

Canadian Records for Women's Outdoor Track and Field

Event	Time/ Distance	Athlete	Date (dd/ mm/yyyy)	Location
100m	10.98	Angela Bailey	06/07/1987	Budapest (Hungary)
200m	22.62	Marita Wiggins	10/07/1983	Edmonton (Canada)
400m	49.91	Jillian Richardson	25/09/1988	Seoul (Korea)
800m	1:58.39	Diane Cummins	02/09/2001	Rieti (Italy)
1000m	2:34.14	Diane Cummins	30/08/2002	Brussels (Belgium)
1500m	4:00.27	Lynn Williams	30/08/1985	Brussels (Belgium)
Mile	4:23.28	Leah Pells	14/08/1996	Zurich (Switzerland)
2000m	5:34.49	Angela Chalmers	04/09/1994	Sheffield (UK)
3000m	8:32.17	Angela Chalmers	23/08/1994	Victoria (Canada)
5000m	14:54.98	Courtney Babcock	30/08/2003	Paris (France)
10,000m	31:44.74	Courtney Babcock	02/05/2003	Palo Alto (U.S.)
Marathon	2:28:36	Silvia Ruegger	06/01/1985	Houston (U.S.)
5km Race Walk (Track)	21:52.95	Pascale Grand	25/06/1990	Belfast (Ireland)
10km Race Walk (Road)	44:26	Janice McCaffrey	11/05/1996	Eisenhüttenstadt (Germany)
10km Race Walk (Track)	44:30.1	Alison Baker	15/05/1993	Bergen (Norway)
20km Race Walk (Road)	1:34:50	Janice McCaffrey	13/08/2000	Victoria (Canada)
100m Hurdles	12.46	Perdita Felicien	19/06/2004	Eugene (U.S.)
400m Hurdles	54.39	Rosey Edeh	31/07/1996	Atlanta (U.S.)
3000m Steeplechase	9:51.1	Carol Henry	01/06/2002	Baton Rouge (U.S.)

Canadian Women Outdoor cont.

Event	Time/Distance	Athlete	Date (dd/mm/yyyy)	Location
4x100m Relay	43.17	Carol Howe	31/07/1976	Montréal (Canada)
		Patty Loverock		
		Joanne McTaggart		
		Marg Bailey		
4x200m Relay	1:33.40	Foy Williams	24/04/2004	Indianapolis (U.S.)
		Lindsey Lochhead		
		Erica Witter		
		Daniella Vega		
4x400m Relay	3:21.21	Charmaine Crooks	11/08/1984	Los Angeles (U.S.)
		Jillian Richardson		
		Molly Killingbeck		
		Marita Payne		
4x800m Relay	8:28.55	Melina Thibedeau	10/05/2003	Burnaby (Canada)
		Katie Vermuelen		
		Heather Henniger		
		Diane Cummins		
4x1500m Relay	18:10.75	Merissa Sexsmith	27/04/2001	Philadelphia (U.S.)
		Rebecca Stallwood		
		Karin Lockhart		
		Megan Metcalfe		
High Jump	1.98m	Debbie Brill	02/09/1984	Rieti (Italy)
Pole Vault	4.52m	Dana Ellis-Butler	18/08/2007	Chula Vista (U.S.)
Long Jump	6.66m	Nicole Devonish	17/05/1996	Lubbock (U.S.)

Canadian Women Outdoor cont.

Event	Time/ Distance	Athlete	Date (dd/ mm/yyyy)	Location
Triple Jump	13.94m	Tabia Charles	29/04/2006	Philadelphia (U.S.)
Shot Put	17.83m	Lieja Tunks	13/06/2007	Arnham (Netherlands)
Discus Throw	62.72m	Carmen Ionescu	23/08/1979	Montréal (Canada)
Hammer Throw	68.60m	Crystal Smith	14/06/2007	Lexington (U.S.)
Javelin Throw	56.06m	Krista Woodward	25/03/2007	Tuscaloosa (U.S.)
Heptathlon	6490 points	Jessica Zelinka	13/09/2008	Beijing Olympics (China)

World Records for Women's Outdoor Track and Field

Event	Time/ Distance	Name	Date (dd/ mm/yyyy)	Location
100m	10.49	Florence Griffith Joyner (USA)	16/07/1988	Indianapolis (U.S.)
200m	21.34	Florence Griffith Joyner (USA)	29/09/1988	Seoul (Korea)
400m	47.60	Marita Koch (EGER)	06/10/1985	Canberra (Australia)
800m	1:53.28	Jarmila Kratochvilova (CZE)	26/07/1983	Munich (Germany)
1000m	2:28.98	Svetlana Masterkova (RUS)	23/08/1996	Brussels (Belgium)
1500m	3:50.46	Qu Yunxia (CHN)	11/09/1993	Beijing (China)
Mile	4:12.56	Svetlana Masterkova (RUS)	14/08/1996	Zurich (Switzerland)
2000m	5:25.36	Sonia O'Sullivan (IRE)	08/07/1994	Edinburgh (Scotland)
3000m	8:06.11	Wang Junxia (CHN)	13/09/1993	Beijing (China)

World Women Outdoor cont.

Event	Time/Distance	Name	Date (dd/mm/yyyy)	Location
5000m	14:11.15	Tirunesh Dibaba (ETH)	06/06/2008	Brussels (Belgium)
10,000m	29:31.78	Wang Junxia (CHN)	08/09/1993	Beijing (China)
Marathon	2:15:25	Paula Radcliffe (GBR)	13/04/2003	London (UK)
5km Race Walk (Track)	20:02.60	Gillian O'Sullivan (IRE)	13/07/2002	Dublin (Ireland)
10km Race Walk(Road)	41:04	Yelena Nikolayeva	20/04/1996	Sochi (Russia)
10km Race Walk (Track)	41:56.23	Nadezhda Ryashkina (USSR)	24/07/1990	Seattle (U.S.)
20km Race Walk (Road)	1:25:41	Olimpiada Ivanova	07/08/2005	Helsinki (Finland)
100m Hurdles	12.21	Yordanka Donkova (BUL)	20/08/1988	Stara Zagora (Bulgaria)
400m Hurdles	52.34	Yuliya Pechonikina (RUS)	08/08/2003	Tula (Russia)
3000m Steeplechase	8:58.81	Gulnara Samitova (RUS)	17/08/2008	Beijing (China)
4x100m Relay	41.37	Silke Gladisch	06/10/1985	Canberra (Australia)
		Sabine Rieger		
		Ingrid Auerswald		
		Marlies Gohr (EGER)		
4x200m Relay	1:27.46	Latasha Jenkins	29/04/2000	Philadelphia (U.S.)
		Latasha Colander-Richardson		
		Nanceen Perry		
		Marion Jones (USA)		

World Women Outdoor cont.

Event	Time/ Distance	Name	Date (dd/ mm/yyyy)	Location
4x400m Relay	3:15.17	Tatyana Ledovskaya	01/10/1988	Seoul (Korea)
		Olga Nazarova		
		Mariya Pinigina		
		Olga Bryzgina (USSR)		
4x800m Relay	7:50.17	Nadezhda Olizarenko	05/08/1984	Moscow (USSR)
		Lyubov Gurina		
		Lyudmila Borisova		
		Irina Podyalovskaya (USSR)		
4x1500m Relay	17:09.75	Natalie Harvey	25/6/2000	London (England)
		Georgia Clarke		
		Kate Richardson		
		Sarah Jamieson (AUS)		
High Jump	2.09m	Stefka Kostadinova (BUL)	30/08/1987	Rome (Italy)
Pole Vault	5.05m	Yelena Isinbayeva (RUS)	18/08/2008	Beijing (China)
Long Jump	7.52m	Galina Chistyakova (USSR)	11/06/1988	Leningrad (USSR)
Triple Jump	15.50m	Inessa Kravets (UKR)	10/08/1995	Göteborg (Sweden)
Shot Put	22.63m	Natalya Lisovskaya (USSR)	07/06/1987	Moscow (USSR)
Discus Throw	76.80m	Gabriele Reinsch (EGER)	09/07/1988	Neubrandenburg (Germany)

World Women Outdoor cont.

Event	Time/ Distance	Name	Date (dd/ mm/yyyy)	Location
Hammer Throw	77.80m	Tatyana Lysenko (RUS)	15/08/2006	Tallin (Estonia)
Javelin Throw	72.28m	Barbora Spotakova (CZE)	13/9/2008	Stuttgart (Germany)
Heptathlon	7291 points	Jackie Joyner-Kersee (USA)	24/09/1988	Seoul (Korea)

Canadian Records for Women's Indoor Track and Field

Event	Time/ Distance	Athlete	Date (dd/ mm/yyyy)	Location
50m	6.05	Philomena Mensah	13/02/2000	Lievin (France)
60m	7.02	Philomena Mensah	11/02/2000	Ghent (Belgium)
200m	23.32	Angela Bailey	15/01/1984	Sherbrooke (Canada)
400m	51.69	Jillian Richardson	22/02/1992	Birmingham (UK)
800m	2:00.66	Diane Cummins	28/02/2003	Karlsruhe (Germany)
1000m	2:38.24	Diane Cummins	23/02/2003	Lievin (France)
1500m	4:08.18	Carmen Douma-Hussar	06/03/2004	Budapest (Hungary)
Mile	4:27.77	Lynn Williams	18/01/1986	Los Angeles (U.S.)
3000m	8:50.80	Lynn Williams	07/03/1987	Indianapolis (U.S.)
5000m	15:37.02	Kathy Butler	08/02/1997	Indianapolis (U.S.)
50m Hurdles	6.78	Keturah Anderson	21/02/1999	Lievin (France)
60m Hurdles	7.75	Perdita Felicien	07/03/2004	Budapest (Hungary)
3000m Race Walk	12:32.34	Ann Peel	04/03/1989	Budapest (Hungary)

Canadian Women Indoor cont.

Event	Time/ Distance	Athlete	Date (dd/ mm/yyyy)	Location
4x200m Relay	1:37.11	Venolym Clarke	10/03/1983	Toronto (Canada)
		Lisa Laughton		
		Kelly Dinsmore		
		Irma Grant		
4x400m Relay	3:36.03	Karlene Haughton	05/03/2000	Glasgow (Scotland)
		Foy Williams		
		Candace Jones		
		Naabiama Salifu		
4x800m Relay	8:41.66	Tania Jones	11/03/1988	Winnipeg (Canada)
		Robyn Meagher		
		Brenda Shackleton		
		Trish Wellman		
High Jump	1.99m	Debbie Brill	23/01/1982	Edmonton (Canada)
Pole Vault	4.41m	Dana Buller	03/02/2007	Albuquerque (U.S.)
Long Jump	6.57m	Krysha Bayley	21/01/2005	Clemnson (U.S.)
Triple Jump	14.02m	Tabia Charles	25/02/2000	Notre Dame (U.S.)
Shot Put	17.02m	Carmen Ionesco	09/03/1979	Montréal (Canada)
Pentath- lon	4550 points	Jill Ross-Giffen	20/02/1982	Canyon (U.S.)

World Records for Women's Indoor Track and Field

Event	Time/ Distance	Athlete	Date (dd/ mm/yyyy)	Location
50m	5.96	Irina Privalova (RUS)	09/02/1995	Madrid (Spain)
60m	6.92	Irina Privalova (RUS)	11/02/1993	Madrid (Spain)
200m	21.87	Merlene Ottey (JAM)	13/02/1993	Lievin (France)
400m	49.59	Jarmila Kratochvilova (CZE)	07/03/1982	Milan (Italy)
800m	1:55.82	Jolanda Ceplak (SLO)	03/03/2002	Vienna (Austria)
1000m	2:30.94	Maria Mutola (MOZ)	25/02/1999	Stockholm (Sweden)
1500m	3:57.71	Yelena Soboleva (RUS)	09/03/2008	Valencia (Spain)
Mile	4:17.14	Doina Melinte (ROM)	09/02/1990	East Rutherford (U.S.)
3000m	8:23.72	Meseret Defar (ETH)	03/02/2007	Stuttgart (Germany)
5000m	14:27.42	Tirunesh Dibaba (ETH)	27/01/2007	Roxbury Crossing (U.S.)
50m Hurdles	6.58	Cornelia Oschkenat (EGER)	20/02/1988	Berlin (East Germany)
60m Hurdles	7.68	Susanna Kallur (SWE)	10/02/2008	Karlsruhe (Germany)
3000m Race Walk	11:40.33	Claudia Stef (ROM)	30/01/1999	Bucharest (Romania)
4x200m Relay	1:32.41	Yekaterina Kondratyeva	29/01/2005	Glasgow (Scotland)
		Irina Khabarova		
		Yuliya Pechonkia		
		Yuliya Gushchina (RUS)		

World Women Indoor cont.

Event	Time/ Distance	Athlete	Date (dd/ mm/yyyy)	Location
4x400m Relay	3:23.37	Yuliya Gushchina	28/01/2006	Glasgow (Scotland)
		Olga Kotlyarova		
		Olga Zaytseva		
		Olesya Krasnomovets (RUS)		
4x800m Relay	8:18.54	Anna Balaksina	11/02/2007	Volgograd (Russia)
		Natalya Pantelyeva		
		Anna Emashova		
		Olesya Chumakova (RUS)		
High Jump	2.08m	Kajsa Bergqvist (SWE)	04/02/2006	Arnstadt (Germany)
Pole Vault	4.95m	Yelena Isinbayeva (RUS)	16/02/2008	Donets'k (Ukraine)
Long Jump	7.37m	Heike Drechsler (EGER)	13/02/1988	Vienna (Austria)
Triple Jump	15.36m	Tatyana Lebedeva (RUS)	06/03/2004	Budapest (Hungary)
Shot Put	22.50m	Helena Fibingerova (CZE)	19/02/1977	Jablonec (Czechoslovakia)
Pentath- lon	4991 points	Irina Belova (RUS)	15/02/1992	Berlin (Germany)

Boxing

Lennox Lewis

Though many Canadians might not know it, Lennox Lewis is a Canadian citizen who started his boxing career in southern Ontario. Born in London, England, his family relocated to Kitchener, Ontario, in 1977 when Lewis was 12 years old. Attending the Cameron Heights Collegiate Institute, Lewis excelled at many sports but made a career out of his skill in boxing. Coached by Arnie Boehm, Lewis was led to a dominating amateur record of 75–7 with 58 KOs. Only six years after he moved to Canada, he was the World Amateur Junior champion in 1983. In this same year, he was also named Athlete of the Year in Canada. Representing his country as a super heavyweight at the 1984 Olympics in Los Angeles, Lewis made it to the quarter-finals, where he lost to American Tyrell Biggs and ended up in fifth place. In the hopes of winning a gold medal at the next Olympics, Lewis stayed in Canada and trained as an amateur until the 1988 Summer Games in Seoul, South Korea. Despite fighting with a broken thumb, Lewis found what he had been waiting for: the gold in the super heavyweight boxing division, defeating future world champion Riddick Bowe by a second-round technical knockout. With this victory, Lewis took home Canada's first gold medal in boxing in over 50 years.

In between his Olympic bouts representing Canada, Lewis also won the Super Heavyweight Commonwealth Games in 1986 and the North American Super Heavyweight Championship in 1987. Unfortunately for Canada's record books, however, Lewis moved back to England after his gold-medal win in Seoul. Unable to find the financial support in Canada that he needed to turn pro, the contract offered to him in England was too good to pass up. Of the decision, Lewis later said:

> *When I fought under the British flag, it was because of the politics in sport in Canada...I always wanted to fight in Toronto as a pro, but it never happened. I got to fight in New York and at Caesar's Palace in Las Vegas, but it never happened here, close to where I grew up. That will always be a gap.*

Once Lewis made the choice to relocate to England, his fight roster in the years to come was filled with the biggest names in boxing. In 1992, Lewis knocked out fellow Canadian Donavan "Razor" Ruddock in two rounds for the top contender's position in the World Boxing Council (WBC). This win ended up awarding Lewis more than he originally thought: after Lewis' Seoul opponent for the Olympic gold, Bowe, became the world heavyweight champion by defeating Evander Holyfield, Bowe refused to fight Lewis again, as Bowe had previously said he would. As a result, Bowe's title was declared vacant, and in 1993, the WBC declared Lewis the new champion.

Lewis went on to defend his belt three times before facing a technical-knockout loss to Oliver McCall in 1994. Lewis' next chance for the belt came in 1997 in Las Vegas—a bout that put him up against McCall once again. In a strange twist, McCall refused to fight the fourth and fifth rounds and began to cry in the ring. As a result, the fight was stopped, and Lewis was awarded the win.

Nicknamed "The Lion," Lewis defended his title once again in 2002, this time against Mike Tyson. It turned out to be an easy victory for Lewis; at the end of the eighth round, he knocked out Tyson with a right hand that sent his opponent sprawling to the mat. This hype-heavy televised fight was the highest-grossing event in pay-per-view history, until it was surpassed by the Oscar De La Hoya and Floyd Mayweather Jr. fight of 2007. The Lewis-Tyson fight was also the biggest sporting event ever held in Memphis, Tennessee.

Lewis retired from the ring in 2004, and his pro record was 41 wins, 2 losses and 1 draw, with 32 wins by knockout. Along with Gene Tunney and Rocky Marciano, he is one of three world heavyweight champions to retire with no unavenged defeats. The choice to withdraw from the ring was never second-guessed by Lewis:

I always ask myself why old heavyweights come back, but I plan to stay out of the ring. I've got a new life now, a new future. There's a lot more to Lennox Lewis than just being a boxer. I am very sure about my decision.

In 2008, Lewis became the 17th boxer to be inducted into Canada's Sports Hall of Fame, and in 2009, in his first year of eligibility, was also inducted into the International Boxing Hall of Fame.

Sam Langford

While many outside of the world of boxing might not know who Sam Langford is, those who are familiar with his accomplishments have gone so far as to call him the greatest pound-for-pound fighter in history. Born in Weymouth Falls, Nova Scotia, in 1886, Langford was a descendent of escaped slaves who had won their freedom in the 18th century by defeating their masters during the American Revolution. Langford's time in Canada was short-lived, however, because, at age 12, he ran away from home in 1898 after the death of his mother. Leaving behind a job in the Nova Scotia woods that earned him $5 a month, Langford ran to Digby, Nova Scotia, then Grand Manan, New Brunswick, and crossed over into the United States, taking up residence in Cambridge, Massachusetts. Working his way to Boston, he ended up employed as a janitor in the boxing gym The Lenox Athletic Club; thus began his career as the Greatest Fighter Nobody Knows, as dubbed by ESPN.

While a janitor at the gym, Langford eventually became a sparring partner for some of the pros who trained there. Eventually entering fights of his own, he became the amateur featherweight champion at the age of 15 and turned pro soon afterward. Within a year, at age 16, Langford was a welterweight, and by 18 years old was ready to move into the big leagues. Unfortunately, the racial views of the time repeatedly denied him the chance to fight for a pro championship. White boxers often avoided going up against black boxers, especially those as talented as Langford turned out to be.

In 1903, Langford beat lightweight champion Joe Gans in 15 rounds in a non-title matchup. A year later Langford went up against light heavyweight champion Joe Walcott in a controversial fight that Walcott won—a bout in which many thought Langford should have taken the victory. This was the only chance Langford had in his entire career to win an official world championship. Heartbreak came again in 1906 when Langford fought Jack Johnson, the man who later became the first black heavyweight champion of the world. Langford lost to Johnson in a 15-round decision and, once declared champion, Johnson refused to let Langford have a chance at the title for fear of losing it. Because of racism, Langford often ended up in bouts against other black boxers; it's estimated that Langford fought Joe Jeanette and Sam McVey 13 times and Harry Willis 18 times.

Langford's reputation as a hard-to-beat pugilist only grew stronger in the years to come, and in 1910, mirroring Johnson four years earlier, middleweight champion Stanley Ketchel also wouldn't put his title down against Langford. Seeking new competition, Langford eventually travelled abroad to England, Australia, France, Mexico and back to his native Canada. It was internationally that Langford found true success, holding titles in England, Spain and Mexico.

Despite standing at five-foot-seven and averaging between 170 and 180 pounds during his career, Langford was an intimidating figure. According to Kevin Smith, author of *The*

*Sundowners: The History of the Black Prizefighter
1870–1930*:

> *People always talk about his arms being so long,
> but reach is a deceptive measurement because it
> includes the breadth of your shoulders. And if you
> look at Langford from the back, his shoulders were
> just tremendously broad. He was a freak of nature,
> there's no doubt. He was all torso and arms, and
> a big, thick neck. He was kind of like [Mike] Tyson
> with longer arms and broader shoulders, if you
> can believe that, and a little bit shorter.*

Indeed, Langford scored more knockouts in his
career than George Foreman and Tyson combined.

Known by the boxing world as the Boston Ter-
ror or The Boston Tar Baby, by the height of his
career in 1917, Langford began to suffer in the
ring due to an injury in his left eye that caused
him to lose vision in it. He refused to give up
boxing and continued to fight for seven more
years. Relying on his hearing, knowledge of foot
patterns and his right eye, he won his last fight in
1923 in Mexico to claim the heavyweight title.
He later recalled:

> *I went down to Mexico…with this here left eye
> completely gone and the right eye just seeing
> shadows. It was a cataract. They matched me up
> with Kid Savage for the title. I was bluffing*

through that I could see but I gave myself away.
They bet awful heavy on The Kid when the word
got round. I just felt my way around and then,
wham, I got home. He forgot to duck and I was the
heavyweight champion of Mexico.

Langford ended up completely blind and penniless in Harlem, New York City, until 1944 when sports writer Al Laney of the *New York Herald Tribune* discovered him all over again, publishing a series of articles about him and his deteriorated condition. Money flowed in from loyal fans that eventually funded eye surgery for Langford. He went on to live a comfortable life from the sports writers' fund set up in his name. Langford died in 1956 while living with his daughter in Cambridge.

Upon his death, it is believed he fought at least 293 times, won at least 167 bouts against 38 defeats, had 37 draws, 48 no-decisions, 3 no-contests and scored at least 117 knockouts. His knockouts alone rank Langford in the top-10 boxers of all time. A year before his death, esteemed boxing writer Nat Fleischer named Langford the seventh-best heavyweight of all time. Langford was also inducted into the Ring Boxing Hall of Fame that same year (1955) and joined the ranks of the International Boxing Hall of Fame in 1990. Canada didn't forget about Langford, either, and Weymouth Falls has a school named after him, along with a plaque put up in his name in the community hall. In 1996, the Historic Sites and Monuments Board of Canada recognized Langford's contribution to Canadian history, and in 1999, he was voted number one in Nova Scotia's Top 10 Male Athletes of the 20th Century.

Basketball

The Edmonton Grads

The best basketball team in the world during their time in competition, the Edmonton Grads female basketball team was founded in 1915 after the senior basketball team at McDougall Commercial High School in Edmonton, Alberta, wanted to continue competing following graduation. Their coach J. Percy Page agreed to stay on with the team outside of the high school, and once in competition the newly named Edmonton Grads began their domination of women's basketball.

During the years of the team's existence from 1915 to 1940, they had an incredible record of 502 wins and only 20 losses. No other team in pro or amateur North American sports history has compiled a winning percentage that has come close to matching what the Grads achieved. Apart from dominating the North American basketball circuit, the Grads were also unbeatable on international courts. At four consecutive Olympic Games between 1924 and 1936, the Grads won all 27 of their games and outscored their opponents 1863 to 297. This amazing record went unrecognized in the medal counts as women's basketball did not become an official sport in the Olympics until the 1976 Games in Montréal. The Grads squad disbanded in 1940 because of World War II, but they left basketball history with an unprecedented 108 local, provincial, national and international titles, reigning supreme as the world's best female team for an unbeatable 17 years in a row. Dr. James Naismith, inventor of basketball, called the women from Edmonton "the finest basketball team that ever stepped out on a floor."

Cycling
Alison Sydor

Despite not beginning to cycle until the age of 20, Alison Sydor became one of Canada's most decorated athletes in the sport. Born in 1966 in Edmonton, Alberta, it was 1987, in her first year of biochemistry studies at the University of Victoria in BC, when Sydor decided to take up the sport as a pastime. Having dabbled in almost every sport imaginable (she is a former Alberta junior champion in the triathlon) throughout her teenage years, as far as she thought at the time, what was the reason not to try cycling? Sydor found her calling and that year won gold in three cycling disciplines at the Western Canadian Games. Within a year, in 1988, she was on the national team. Sydor faltered at the World Road Championships in Japan in 1990, coming dead last, but three years later, in 1991, redeemed herself and became the first Canadian woman to win a World Championship medal (bronze) in the individual road race competition. Choosing to concentrate on her mountain biking skills for the remainder of the year, she also won the Grundig World Cup and the prestigious Tour de l'Aude in 1991.

By 1992, Sydor was ranked the third-best road racer in the world, but fell short of a medal at the Barcelona Olympics that year, placing 12th in road racing. Of her loss there, Sydor later said:

I've been a bike racer since 1987 and mentally, physically and technically I am approaching my best years in this sport. I didn't feel that in Barcelona. I still felt I was learning a lot as an athlete and I wasn't ready to take the pressure and be one of the favourites.

She did, however, capture the silver medal in mountain biking at the 1992 World Championships in Québec. Officially turning pro in 1993, Sydor went on to win the World Championships again in 1994, 1995 and 1996, claim gold at the 1995 Pan American Games and win silver in mountain biking at the 1996 Atlanta Olympics. Sydor came fifth at the Sydney Olympics in 2000 and fourth at Athens in 2004.

From 1992 to 2004, Sydor also won five silver medals and four bronze at various other world championships. In her career she won 17 World Cup races and for 13 consecutive years—1992–2004—never finished outside of the top five at the World Championships.

Her accolades among Canadians and Americans alike were never in short supply—she was Canada's top female athlete in 1995 and 1996, was awarded an Order of British Columbia and named one of Canada's cyclists of the century by Canadian Cyclist in 1999, was inducted into the Mountain Bike Hall of Fame in Colorado in 2007 and was part of the Class of 2008 at the British Columbia Sports Hall of Fame induction ceremonies. With stories of races in which Sydor collapsed at the finish line from exhaustion and hypothermia with her foot still in her pedal stirrup to tales of her crossing the finish line with a flat tire, carrying her broken bike to the end, Sydor has never given in to defeat.

Athens was Sydor's final Olympic appearance, and she has spent her time since focused on endurance races and cyclocross. She won the eight-day Cape Epic with her partner Pia Sundstedt in 2008 and came second in the 2007 Canadian Cyclocross Nationals. Regardless of how she fares in future events, Sydor has made her mark in Canada as the most accomplished mountain-bike racer ever. As she said after a bronze-medal win in 1998, "I think experience still counts for something out here."

Steve Bauer

Raised in Fenwick, Ontario, Steve Bauer's hometown later became part of his cycling nickname, the "Fenwick Flash." Starting out in the sport as a member of the St. Catharines Cycling Club, he officially began his amateur career on the Canadian national cycling team in 1977, competing in Team Pursuit. He remained on the team for seven years, taking first place in the National Road Race Championship from 1981 to 1983. Bauer turned pro in 1984 after placing second in the men's cycling road race at the Olympics in Los Angeles that year. It didn't take long for Bauer to excel in the world of professional road racing, and in only his second pro race—the World Professional Road Race in Barcelona—he came in third, a feat unheard of in the cycling world. This was only a prelude to Bauer's accomplishments, which included a fourth-place finish in the 1988 Tour de France. He won the first stage of this Tour and wore the coveted yellow jersey for five days—singling him out as only the second Canadian to ever wear the jersey. And although he finished 27th in the 1990 Tour de France, Bauer still managed to wear the yellow jersey for nine days.

Unfortunately, Bauer's career was not without its difficulties. At the 1988 World Championships, he collided with fellow competitor and 1984 world champion Claude Criquielion as both men were coming into the finish for the gold medal. Bauer was disqualified and then sued by Criquielion for $1.5 million in damages on the charge of assault. After five years in court, Bauer was acquitted.

Also, the year after the Criquielion incident, with only five kilometres to go in the World Championship, Bauer was cursed with a flat tire. Up until that point, Bauer said he was riding the best race of his life. Facing a third heartbreak, in the 1995 Tour de France, Bauer's teammate Fabio Casartelli died in a crash during the Tour.

Bauer competed in his final Olympic Games in 1996 in Atlanta, coming 41st. He knew his time was up, saying:

Not too many guys my age are doing this. You have to be realistic. I'm still going well...there are some races when you have [a] shot...I won't miss it. It's too hard. It's too hard to do this anymore.

Canada's highest-ever ranked professional road racer and the only Canadian to lead the Tour de France on two separate occasions, with only two other Canadians following him into the Tour, Bauer announced in October 1996 that he was retiring. But, in one way or the other, Bauer never left the world of cycling. In 1997, he co-launched Steve Bauer Bike Tours in the Niagara region in Ontario, which specialized in high-quality bicycle tours and events for different cycling fitness levels and interests. The company now focuses on more exclusive international trips, with visits to the Tour de France for hardcore cycling enthusiasts.

In 2009, Bauer is still active and has announced the debut of his Planet Energy Pro Cycling Team—a team uniquely made up of Canadians only. With the goal of eventually becoming the first all-Canadian team to compete in the Tour de France, the team will participate in its first race in Cuba, with others scheduled in Mexico,

California, Uruguay and Canada in 2009. "We [Canada] need to have more of these teams," says Bauer. "We have athletes who can compete at this level. We just need the sponsorship and support to make it happen."

Curt Harnett

Hailing from Thunder Bay, Ontario, Curt Harnett's heart originally lay with hockey, and he only began cycling as a way to stay in shape in the off-season. He soon realized where his true calling was and went on to compete as a cyclist in four Olympic Games, winning one silver medal and two bronze.

Harnett stormed onto the cycling scene as a teenager with his debut at the 1984 Los Angeles Olympics, where he claimed his first medal, a silver in the 1000-metre time trial. His finish was only three one-hundredths-of-a-second behind the gold-medal winner, Germany's Fredy Schmidtke.

Highlights along the way to his third and final Olympic Games in Atlanta in 1996 include two silver medals at the Commonwealth Games in the match sprint, a bronze finish in this event at the 1992 Barcelona Olympics, two second-place finishes in the World Championships and a Goodwill Games gold. Not to be forgotten, however, is his amazing performance when he broke the world record for the 200-metre time trial in 1995 in Bogota, Colombia. He was the first man to complete the event in under 10 seconds (9.865), averaging a speed of nearly 73 kilometres per hour, a record that stood for 11 years.

Harnett participated in his last race in 1996 at the Atlanta Olympics and ended up in a close battle for bronze in the match sprint against his friend Gary Niewand of Australia. As Harnett said afterward, he couldn't have wrapped up his career in a better way:

As much as I was disappointed that I wasn't going for gold, I was really enjoying myself and living in the moment. It was the final race of my career and it was the best race I ever had in my life.

Harnett ended up with third place, edging out Niewand, and later famously said, "It's time to get a haircut and get a real job."

And he did, attending the Sydney and Athens Olympics as a commentator for the CBC and becoming involved with many sports organizations and charities. The only cyclist in Canadian history to win three Olympic medals, Harnett was inducted into the Canadian Olympic Hall of Fame in 2006, and of getting out for a bike ride since his retirement, he has said, "I'm a fair-weather rider. If I'm going for a serious bike ride, it's got to be nice outside."

Jocelyn Lovell

While casual cycling fans might not recognize the name Jocelyn Lovell, many diehard cyclists and sports historians view him as being responsible for bringing Canadian cycling back into the international spotlight in the 1960s and '70s. Born in England and moving to southern Ontario when he was a little boy, Lovell never used a coach, preferring to create and execute his own training programs. Fully emerging as a force to be reckoned with at the 1970 Commonwealth Games in Edinburgh, Lovell won gold, silver and bronze medals, which were Canada's first cycling medals in 32 years. He continued to dominate at the Commonwealth Games, winning five cycling events in 1974 and at the 1978 Edmonton Games taking gold three times and breaking records in each event. He became the first man to achieve such a feat. The 1000-metre time trial was his best event, and he defended it heartily throughout his career, setting a record that stood for 28 years. In contending for titles in various events, he would dare fellow competitors to keep pace with his killer tactics, then "crack their legs" by attacking the pack when they were tired.

With such ferocity, Lovell competed at the Munich and Montréal Olympics in 1972 and 1976, but injuries barred him any podium finishes. Armed with a silver from the 1978 World Championships, however, Lovell was ready for the 1980 Moscow Olympics. But, because of the boycott, Canada would never know what could have been—in more ways than one. While training in 1983 in Mississauga, Ontario, Lovell was hit by a dump truck and dragged for 30 metres. He has been a quadriplegic ever since.

Lovell held the world record in the 1000-metre time trial until 1999, and no other Commonwealth cyclist has won more medals in the Games. Inducted into Canada's Sports Hall of Fame in 1985, Lovell is the long-time head of an international advocacy group that promotes research into spinal-cord injuries and curing paralysis. He still thinks about cycling, though, saying it would "be great to be back in there, cracking a few legs."

Smallbore Shooting
Gimour Boa and Gerard Ouellette

Smallbore shooting is not one of the most popular events on the Olympic calendar, but Canadians have done well in the event in the past. Canada's best-ever showing came at the 1956 Olympics in Melbourne where, in the smallbore-prone event, Canada's Gilmour Boa and Gerard Ouellette were expected to finish on the podium. Boa already held the world record in the event with 598 points and managed to tie it in the final round. Ouellette shot next and managed a perfect 600, with 60 bull's eyes in a row. He went home happy with a gold medal around his neck, and Canadian teammate Boa ended up in a respectable third place. It was later found out, however, that the course Ouellette and Boa competed on was approximately 1.5 metres too short, so while Ouellette still owns his gold medal, his name is not listed beside the official Olympic record in his sport.

Paralympics
Chantal Petitclerc

Chantal Petitclerc lost the use of her legs when she was 13 years old. Playing on the family farm in

Saint-Marc-des-Carrières, Québec, a heavy barn door fell on her and changed her life forever. Petit-clerc embraced her new position in a wheelchair and soon changed the face of the Paralympics.

Petitclerc first took up the sport of wheelchair racing when she met Pierre Pomerleau, a Paralympics coach who encouraged her to take up the sport. She quickly discovered she had a natural ability to wheelchair-race and was soon at the top of the standings in provincial and national competition. Petitclerc made the jump to the international stage in the early 1990s, and in 1992 competed in her first Paralympic Games in Barcelona. She took home two bronze medals and improved in the Olympic-medal standings in subsequent Games, with three silver and two gold in 1996 in Atlanta, two silver and two gold in 2000 in Sydney, five gold in Athens in 2004 and five gold in Beijing in 2008. In 2008, Petitclerc was named Female Athlete of Year at the Canadian Sports Awards and by the Canadian Press.

Judo
Doug Rogers

Judo first made its appearance on the Olympic calendar at the 1964 Tokyo Games. It was expected that the Japanese, who had created the martial art centuries ago, would walk away with at least one gold medal, but to everyone's surprise, a lone Canadian fighter in the heavyweight class posed a threat to Japan's expectations.

Truro, Nova Scotia native Doug Rogers did not have the perceived pedigree of Japan's top competitor, Isao Inokuma. But studying for years under the tutelage of one of judo's greatest competitors, Masahiko Kimura, Rogers was more than ready for any challenge.

When the heavyweight event in Tokyo got underway, Rogers defeated a Taiwanese opponent in the first round, a Mexican in the second and a Russian in the semifinal to get through to the final round, in which he fought against the formidable Inokuma.

It was an intense battle between two technically skilled judo masters. Fans watched in awe as Rogers had an answer for most of Inokuma's challenges, but in the end the gold was given to the Japanese competitor in a close decision. Rogers walked away with the silver medal, gaining the respect of the Japanese hosts, and went on to later success in the Pan American Games in 1967, taking home the gold in open-class judo and silver in the heavyweight class.

Equestrian
Ian Millar

Born in Halifax, Nova Scotia, Millar is a Canadian and world champion in equestrian show-jumping. In a career that has spanned over three decades, Millar has claimed wins in more than 40 Grand Prix titles, the Show Jumping World Cup, the Spruce Meadow Derby, the Pan American Games and the Show Jumping World Championships. Earning the nickname "Captain Canada" because of his longevity in Canadian sport, Millar holds the North American record for Grand Prix and Derby wins. Most recently, at the 2008 Beijing Olympic Games—his ninth visit to the Olympics—Millar, at the age of 61, put his first Olympic medal around his neck. Along with teammates Jill Henselwood, Eric Lamaze and Mac Cone, Millar made it to the finals in the team show-jumping event, but lost to the Americans in a jump-off. Riding his horse named In Style, Millar and his team put together a near-flawless run and claimed silver in the event. "Age does not matter unless it matters to you," Millar said after receiving his long-awaited medal.

It is Millar's plan to make it to the 2012 Games in London, which would give him a total of 10 Olympic appearances and break the world record set by Austrian sailor Hubert Raudaschl.

Canadian Athletes Named to Three or More Summer Olympic Teams

Sport	#	Athlete	Years
Equestrian	9	Ian Millar	2008, 2004, 2000, 1996, 1992, 1988, 1984, 1976, 1972
Sailing	7	Evert Bastet	1992, 1988, 1984, 1980, 1976, 1972, 1968
Equestrian	7	James Elder	1984, 1980, 1976, 1972, 1968, 1960, 1956
Equestrian	7	Christilot Hansen Boylen	1992, 1984, 1980, 1976, 1972, 1968, 1964
Shooting	6	John Primrose	1992, 1988, 1984, 1976, 1972, 1968
Rowing	6	Lesley Thompson	2000, 1996, 1992, 1988, 1984, 1980
Shooting	5	Gilmour Boa	1972, 1964, 1960, 1956, 1952
Canoe/Kayak	5	Caroline Brunet	2004, 2000, 1996, 1992, 1988
Athletics	5	Charmaine Crooks	1996, 1992, 1988, 1984, 1980
Shooting	5	George Leary	2000, 1996, 1992, 1988, 1980
Sailing	5	Ross MacDonald	2004, 2000, 1996, 1992, 1988
Shooting	5	Susan Nattrass	2004, 2000, 1992, 1988, 1976
Athletics	5	Alexander Oakley	1976, 1972, 1964, 1960, 1956
Shooting	5	Jules Sobrian	1984, 1980, 1976, 1972, 1968
Wrestling	5	Doug Yeats	1992, 1988, 1984, 1980, 1976
Athletics	4	Katie Anderson	2000, 1996, 1992, 1988
Fencing	4	Jean-Marie Banos	1996, 1992, 1988, 1984
Fencing	4	Jean-Paul Banos	1996, 1992, 1988, 1984
Diving	4	David Bédard	1996, 1992, 1988, 1984
Athletics	4	Tim Berrett	2004, 2000, 1996, 1992
Shooting	4	Sharon Bowes	2000, 1992, 1988, 1984
Athletics	4	Debbie Brill	1984, 1980, 1976, 1972
Fencing	4	Jean-Marc Chouinard	1996, 1992, 1988, 1984
Sailing	4	Richard Clarke	2004, 2000, 1996, 1992
Canoe/Kayak	4	Hugh Fisher	1988, 1984, 1980, 1976
Canoe/Kayak	4	David Ford	2004, 2000, 1996, 1992

Three or More Olympics cont.

Sport	#	Athlete	Years
Athletics	4	Glenroy Gilbert	2000, 1996, 1992, 1988
Canoe/Kayak	4	Stephen Giles	2004, 2000, 1996, 1992
Judo	4	Nicolas Gill	2004, 2000, 1996, 1992
Equestrian	4	Robin Hahn	1976, 1972, 1968, 1956
Cycling	4	Curt Harnett	1996, 1992, 1988, 1984
Athletics	4	Abigail Hoffman	1976, 1972, 1968, 1964
Athletics	4	Ben Johnson	1992, 1988, 1984, 1980
Rowing	4	Silken Laumann	1996, 1992, 1988, 1984
Athletics	4	Mark McKoy	1992, 1988, 1984, 1980
Judo	4	Joseph Meli	1988, 1984, 1980, 1976
Basketball	4	Romel Meli Raffin	1988, 1984, 1980, 1976
Shooting	4	Jean-François Senécal	1996, 1992, 1988, 1984
Rowing	4	Tricia Smith	1988, 1984, 1980, 1976
Athletics	4	Bruny Surin	2000, 1996, 1992, 1988
Cycling	4	Alison Sydor	2004, 2000, 1996, 1992
Swimming	3	Marianne Limpert	2000, 1996, 1992
Swimming	3	Joanne Malar	2000, 1996, 1992
Athletics	3	Janice McCaffrey	2000, 1996, 1992
Athletics	3	Leah Pells	2000, 1996, 1992
Cycling	3	Brian Walton	2000, 1996, 1988

WINTER SPORTS

Speed Skating

Jeremy Wotherspoon

One of Canada's top speed skaters as of 2009, Jeremy Wotherspoon was originally a hockey player who signed up for a power-skating class in order to improve his skills on the ice. As a nine-year-old, this Red Deer, Alberta native discovered his true athletic calling and began his career in speed skating. Competing in both long-track and short-track events, he climbed quickly through the world of junior speed skating (setting 10 junior world records along the way) and moved to Calgary to train with the Canadian National Team when he was only 17. From there, he became a force to be reckoned with in the long-track 500-metre and 1000-metre events and earned the right to call himself a four-time world sprint champion (1999, 2000, 2001 and 2003) and a multiple World Cup overall champion (winning each year from 1998 to 2005 and in 2008 in the 500-metre; and from 1998 to 2002 in the 1000-metre. He also took home a silver medal in the 500-metre at Nagano in 1998.

The 2002 World Sprint Championships made up Wotherspoon's best competitions in his career, with wins in three out four distances. Despite his success on the world stage, he fell at the start of the 500-metre competition at the 2002 Salt Lake City Winter Olympics, putting him out of medal contention. He also placed 13th in the 1000-metre at Salt Lake, much farther back than the world expected. December 2003 saw Wotherspoon on top again when he claimed the 49th victory of his career, crowning him the most successful male speed skater in World Cup history. As of 2009, Wotherspoon has 67 World Cup wins. His 10 World Cup titles—five in the 500-metre and five in the 1000-metre—is a men's record.

Left off the podium at the 2006 Turin Olympics, finishing 9th in the 500-metre and 11th in the 1000-metre, Wotherspoon took the next speed-skating season off to gain energy and confidence. He came back with a vengeance in the 2007–08 season, winning every international 500-metre he competed in. However, Wotherspoon fell in the first World Cup event of 2008–09 in Berlin, Germany, and is looking at a season rehabilitating his broken left arm rather than skating to more world titles.

Canada is hopeful the time off in 2009 will give Wotherspoon the same focus and determination his previous 2006–07 break gave him, allowing the speed skater to storm to the top of the podium in Vancouver in 2010. Says Wotherspoon of the upcoming Olympics:

It has been a motivation for me to keep competing [because] it is in Canada. Everyone I know who has competed in the Olympics in their country has said it's an incredible experience. It'll be the most unique event I've ever had a chance to be at...and a great way to culminate my career.

Record-breaking Fact

On March 29, 1998, Canadian speed skater Sylvain Bouchard recorded a time of 1:09.60 in the long-track 1000-metre event in Calgary, Alberta, the first time anyone completed the circuit in under 1:10 seconds.

Denny Morrison

Denny Morrison, Canada's other modern male star in the sport of speed skating, has been honing his craft for a long time. Born in Chetwynd, BC, in 1985, Morrison started speed skating when he was only three years old. Participating in both long- and short-track speed-skating events throughout his childhood and some of his teenage years, Morrison decided to devote himself solely to long-track speed skating. In his first World Cup season in 2005–06, he placed second in the 1500-metre and third in the 1000-metre. He also set a world record with Steven Elm and Arne Dankers in the Team Pursuit in 2005. Morrison's success in this event continued in 2006 with a silver medal at the Turin Winter Olympics. His rookie individual-event attempt at the Olympics fell short of expectations, however, and Morrison left Turin with an 11th-place finish in the 1500-metre and a 19th-place finish in the

1000-metre. He came home from Turin, stating he "skated like a junior again."

Back again in 2007 as the speed skater Canada knew him to be, Morrison won gold in the 1000-metre event at the World Cup finals in Calgary, Alberta. His time of 1:07.24 was a Canadian record, besting fellow Canadian Jeremy Wotherspoon. The 2007 World Cup finals also saw Morrison win a bronze medal in the 1500-metre competition.

At the 2007 World Single Distance Championships, Morrison, in Team Pursuit, set an early personal-best time that broke the old Team Pursuit record previously held by Morrison, Elm and Dankers. First place ended up just out of reach, however, as the Dutch team went on to edge Canada into second place by five-tenths of a second. Morrison also took home bronze in the 1500-metre and 1000-metre events.

The following year, Morrison snagged the gold in the 1500-metre at the World Single Distance Championships in Nagano, and only a week later set a new world record of 1:42:01 in the same event at the ING Finale in Calgary. Morrison's time bested the old world record set by both Shani Davis (who was his main competition at the 2007 World Single Distance Championships) and Erben Wennemars.

"That's pretty cool," Morrison said."The last three years I've been looking up Shani Davis' record… looking at that time and going 'How am I going to beat that?'"

Morrison's podium-worthy international performances have continued into 2009, with gold in the 500-metre, 1000-metre and 1500-metre events. Heading into Vancouver in 2010, Morrison will be following personal routines that have gotten him this far and will take him to his second Olympic Games:

I don't follow superstitions as much as routines. I untie my skates 10 minutes before a race, then I tie them back up five minutes before the race…Untying my skates came about because they are so tight, no blood gets in there.

Record-breaking Fact

Canada holds the world record in the short-track speed-skating relay event; Charles Hamelin, F.L. Tremblay, Steve Robillard and Mathieu Turcotte set the bar at 6:39.990 in 2005 in Beijing.

Catriona Le May-Doan

The first and only Canadian individual to successfully defend a gold medal at any Olympic

Games, as well as the female once dubbed the "fastest woman on ice," Catriona Le May-Doan has unequivocally cemented her place in Canada's speed-skating record books. Born in Saskatoon, Saskatchewan, Le May-Doan's career started in the 1980s when she first competed at the Canada Winter Games in 1983 at the age of 13, where she won a bronze medal in short-track speed skating. She also competed at the same Games in 1987, taking home a silver and bronze medal. In addition to her speed-skating success in the '80s, Le May-Doan competed as a hurdler at the Canada Summer Games in 1993. Her participation in these Games gave her the distinct privilege of becoming one of only a few Canadians to have taken part in both a Winter and Summer Canada Games.

Her phenomenal career in speed skating, however, truly began at the 1998 Nagano Winter Olympics. It was there that Le May-Doan won her first Olympic gold medal in the long-track 500-metre event in record Olympic time. While at Nagano, she also won a bronze medal in the long-track 1000-metre competition. In addition to her performances in Japan, she completed the 1998 speed-skating season first overall in World Cup standings in the 500-metre and 1000-metre events. She finished at the top of the World Cup standings in the 500-metre again in 1999.

Continuing to dominate the standings, it was no surprise that in 2002 at the Salt Lake City Olympics she took gold for the second time in the 500-metre, breaking her own Olympic record. As the first Canadian to defend a gold medal at any Olympic Games, she later said:

> *Nobody did it in Canada before. I didn't know that until afterwards…It's difficult to defend. I was proud to defend, but it was not easy. There was a lot of pressure.*

In this amazing year for Le May-Doan, she was champion of the 500-metre event in the Worlds, Olympics and World Cup.

Overall, Le May-Doan broke 13 world records in her career, was the recipient of the 2002 Lou Marsh Award as Canada's Athlete of the Year, was awarded the Canadian Female Athlete of the Year Award three times, was the first woman to break the 38-second barrier in the 500-metre, is the only female with eight consecutive world records in one distance (500-metre), is an Officer of the Order of Canada, was inducted into the Canadian Sports Hall of Fame in 2005 and still holds the Olympic record in the 500-metre going into 2010 in Vancouver. Le May-Doan retired in 2003 but is still active in the athletic community— she was a member of the official Canadian contingent when Vancouver was chosen as the site of the 2010 Olympics. She was also one of the CBC colour commentators for speed skating during the 2006 Turin Olympics.

Cindy Klassen

The first Canadian to win five medals at a single Winter Olympics, Cindy Klassen is one of Canada's top Olympic stars. She, like Jeremy Wotherspoon, is a Winnipeg, Manitoba native who began her ice-skating career as a hockey player. Klassen also took part in lacrosse and in-line skating, participating in the 1994 Commonwealth Games on the women's lacrosse team and in the 1999 Pan American Games as an in-line skater. Hockey remained her most serious sport, however, and Klassen played for the Canadian National Youth Team in her teenage years. Luckily for Canada, when she was not selected for the 1998 Winter Olympic team going to Nagano, she switched her sights to speed skating. This proved to be a life-altering decision for Klassen. In 2002 in her first Olympic competition at Salt Lake City, she took home the bronze medal in the long-track 3000-metre event. Following that in 2003, she finished second overall at the World Sprint Championships and also became the first Canadian in 27 years to win the overall title at the

World Allround Speed Skating Championships. With both of these wins, Klassen marked the first time in 15 years a speed skater had placed on the overall podium in both events in the same year.

Soon afterward, near the end of 2003, Klassen suffered a serious injury, falling during training and colliding with another skater. Klassen hit the other athlete's skate and ended up with 12 cut tendons in her right arm. Once back in competition in 2005, however, it was as if Klassen hadn't even skipped a beat—she won the 1500-metre World Cup title for the second time (2003 was the first) and broke the world record with a time of 1:51.79. Klassen was also a double-gold medalist that year at the World Championships in the 1500-metre and 3000-metre events.

Such a comeback was child's play compared to her unparalleled performance at the Turin Winter Olympics in 2006. Klassen set a record in becoming the first Canadian to win five medals at a single Winter Olympics. She took home gold in the 1500-metre, silver in the 1000-metre and Team Pursuit and bronze in the 5000-metre and 3000-metre. Of her 1500-metre gold-medal win, Klassen said, "The last two laps were really hard, but I wasn't giving up my hopes [for gold]. I'm really lucky to have trained in Calgary and be a Canadian."

It was at Turin that she was also called "the woman of the Games" by International Olympic Committee president Jacques Rogge. Klassen's five wins, in combination with her bronze in Salt Lake City in 2002, make her the most decorated Canadian Olympic athlete in history. But Klassen's amazing 2006 run was not over: she also took home the overall World Cup title in the 3000-metre and won the World Allround Championships with gold in four distances. Topping it off was her 2006 Lou Marsh Award as Canadian Athlete of the Year.

As of 2009, Klassen holds the current women's world records in the 1000-metre, 1500-metre and 3000-metre events. She is also recognized as the holder of the most lucrative endorsement deal ever given to a Canadian amateur athlete— her $1-million contract with Manitoba Telecom Services was nailed down after her amazing performance in Turin in 2006.

All is not yet over for Klassen. After recovering from knee surgery on both legs in 2008, she is expected to return to the World Cup circuit in the fall of 2009 and compete in the Vancouver Olympic Games in 2010. "Being one year out, it seems the hype is going to get a little bigger. I think that motivates us and drives all of us to get ready for 2010," Klassen has said.

Gaétan Boucher

When Gaétan Boucher began speed skating in the late 1960s, there were little to no facilities in Canada where he could practice. At that time, Canada was well behind the rest of the world in speed-skating advancements. For most of his career, Boucher was forced to practice in rinks designed specifically for hockey or to live in Europe and practice on their artificial ice ovals. As Canada was to see, such obstacles did not deter the determined skater from Charlesbourg, Québec.

Boucher began to make a name for himself in the late 1970s, appearing at the 1976 Olympic Winter Games in Innsbruck, Austria, but he was young and unable to keep up with the other world-class athletes. Four years later, the story did not remain the same, and at the 1980 Olympics in Lake Placid, Boucher took home the first Canadian men's medal in speed skating since 1952 by winning the silver in the 1000-metre event. One year after his silver-medal win, Boucher set a new world record in the 1000-metre with a time of 1:13.29, as well as in the men's sprint in all-around points with 148.785.

Boucher returned to the Olympic stage in 1984 in Sarajevo, where he walked away with three medals. In his first race, the 500-metre sprint,

Boucher finished third. The 500-metre event wasn't Boucher's specialty, though, and he was ready to take gold in the 1000-metre race and become the first Canadian to win first place in an Olympic speed-skating event. Conditions at the outdoor speed-skating arena in Sarajevo were less than ideal in a city plagued by some of the worst air-pollution levels in Europe. A difficult circumstance for some athletes, Boucher drew on his earlier experiences of training on poor ice surfaces and triumphed over Russian competitor Sergey Khlebnikov to win the 1000-metre gold medal. Three days later, Boucher beat Khlebnikov again, but this time in the 1500-metre event. In 1984, Boucher claimed the record for the most medals won by a Canadian at a single Olympics, and he was awarded the Lou Marsh Trophy for outstanding Canadian Athlete of the Year. Boucher's final Olympic appearance was in 1988 in Calgary, where he did not medal but received a standing ovation from his many Canadian fans in recognition of his accomplishments.

Record-breaking Fact

In a sport traditionally dominated by Québec-born athletes, Michael Gilday of Yellowknife is one of Canada's quickly rising short-track speed skaters. He holds the world record in the 1000-metre race with a time of 1:23.815, set in Calgary, and he is looking to repeat his incredible performance on the world stage and make it to the 2010 Olympics in Vancouver.

Canadian Men's Short-track Speed-Skating Records

Event	Time	Athlete	Year	Location
500m	41.035	Charles Hamelin	2004	Calgary (Canada)
1000m	1:23.815	Michael Gilday	2007	Calgary (Canada)
1500m	2:10.713	Mathieu Turcotte	2003	Marquette (U.S.)
3000m	4:34.272	Jonathan Guilmette	2003	Beijing (China)
Relay	6:39.990	Charles Hamelin	2005	Beijing (China)
		F.L. Tremblay		
		Steve Robillard		
		Mathieu Turcotte		

World Men's Short-track Speed-Skating Records

Event	Time	Athlete	Year	Location
500m	41.051	Si-Bak Sung (KOR)	2008	Salt Lake City (U.S.)
1000m	1:23.815	Michael Gilday (CAN)	2007	Calgary (Canada)
1500m	2:10.639	Hyun-Soo Ahn (KOR)	2003	Marquette (U.S.)
3000m	4:32.646	Hyun-Soo Ahn (KOR)	2003	Beijing (China)
Relay	6:39.990	Charles Hamelin	2005	Beijing (China)
		F.L. Tremblay		
		Steve Robillard		
		Mathieu Turcotte (CAN)		

Canadian Men's Long-track Speed-skating Records

Event	Time	Athlete	Year	Location
500m	34.03	Jeremy Wotherspoon	2007	Salt Lake City (U.S.)
1000m	1:07.03	Jeremy Wotherspoon	2007	Salt Lake City (U.S.)
1500m	1:42.01	Denny Morrison	2008	Calgary (Canada)
3000m	3:41.96	Arne Dankers	2005	Calgary (Canada)
5000m	6:14.01	Arne Dankers	2005	Salt Lake City (U.S.)
10,000m	13:10.58	Arne Dankers	2005	Heerenveen (Netherlands)
Team Pursuit	3:38.31	Arne Dankers	2007	Salt Lake City (U.S.)
		Denny Morrison		
		Justin Warsylewicz		

World Men's Long-track Speed-skating Records

Event	Time	Athlete	Year	Location
500m	34.03	Jeremy Wotherspoon (CAN)	2007	Salt Lake City (U.S.)
1000m	1:07.00	Pekka Koskela (FIN)	2007	Salt Lake City (U.S.)
1500m	1:42.01	Denny Morrison (CAN)	2008	Calgary (Canada)
3000m	3:37.28	Eskil Ervik (NOR)	2005	Calgary (Canada)
5000m	6:07.48	Sven Kramer (NED)	2007	Calgary (Canada)
10,000m	12:41.69	Sven Kramer (NED)	2007	Salt Lake City (U.S.)
Team Pursuit	3:37.80	Sven Kramer	2007	Salt Lake City (U.S.)
		Carl Verheijen		
		Erben Wennemars (NED)		

Canadian Women's Short-track Speed-Skating Records

Event	Time	Athlete	Year	Location
500m	43.839	Alanna Kraus	2005	Bormio (Italy)
1000m	1:30.823	Amanda Overland	2005	Bormio (Italy)
1500m	2:21.758	Marie-Eve Drolet	2002	Salt Lake City (U.S)
3000m	4:57.389	Raphaele Lemieux	2002	Calgary (Canada)
Relay	4:15.738	Isabelle Charest	2002	Salt Lake City (U.S.)
		Amelie Goulet-Nadon		
		Marie-Eve Drolet		
		Alanna Kraus		

World Women's Short-track Speed-Skating Records

Event	Time	Athlete	Year	Location
500m	43.266	Meng Wang (CHN)	2008	Salt Lake City (U.S.)
1000m	1:30.037	Sun-Yu Jin (KOR)	2005	Bormio (Italy)
1500m	2:16.729	Yang Zhou (CHN)	2008	Salt Lake City (U.S.)
3000m	5:01.976	Eun-Kyung Choi (KOR)	2000	Calgary (Canada)
Relay	4:09.938	Eun-Ju Jung	2008	Salt Lake City (U.S.)
		Seung-Hi Park		
		Sae-Bom Shin		
		Shin-Young Yang (KOR)		

Canadian Women's Long-track Speed-skating Records

Event	Time	Athlete	Year	Location
500m	37.22	Catriona Le May-Doan	2001	Salt Lake City (U.S.)
1000m	1:13.11	Cindy Klassen	2006	Calgary (Canada)
1500m	1:51.79	Cindy Klassen	2005	Salt Lake City (U.S.)
3000m	3:53.34	Cindy Klassen	2006	Calgary (Canada)
5000m	6:48.97	Cindy Klassen	2006	Calgary (Canada)
10,000m	14:19.73	Clara Hughes	2005	Calgary (Canada)
Team Pursuit	2:58.15	Christine Nesbitt	2007	Salt Lake City (U.S.)
		Kristina Groves		
		Shannon Rempel		

World Women's Long-track Speed-skating Records

Event	Time	Athlete	Year	Location
500m	37.02	Jenny Wolf (GER)	2007	Calgary (Canada)
1000m	1:13.11	Cindy Klassen (CAN)	2006	Calgary (Canada)
1500m	1:51.79	Cindy Klassen (CAN)	2005	Salt Lake City (U.S.)
3000m	3:53.34	Cindy Klassen (CAN)	2006	Calgary (Canada)
5000m	6:45.61	Martina Sablikova (CZE)	2007	Salt Lake City (U.S.)
10,000m	13:48.33	Martina Sablikova (CZE)	2007	Calgary (Canada)
Team Pursuit	2:56.04	Daniela Anschutz	2005	Calgary (Canada)
		Annie Friesinger		
		Claudia Pechstein (GER)		

Figure Skating
Kurt Browning

Landing the first-ever quadruple jump in competition, four-time Canadian World Champion Kurt Browning is one of Canada's most talented figure skaters. Born in Rocky Mountain House, Alberta, and later moving to his hometown of Caroline, Alberta, Browning was a hockey player before he was a figure skater; he took to figure skates as a way to hone his skills. His passion for figure skating took over and Browning soon placed first in the 1983 Canadian Novice Championships and 1985 Canadian Junior Championships. He experienced his debut at the Canadian Championships in 1986 and his first World Championship in 1987. By the time the 1988 Worlds in Hungary came around, Browning was well known in the skating community and created even more of a stir when he landed the first quadruple jump ever in competition—an achievement that is listed in the *Guinness Book of Records*. This same year, Browning also competed in his first Olympic Games, in Calgary, but his next claim to fame came in 1990 at the Nations Cup in Germany. Browning awed crowds again by becoming the first to land a triple salchow-triple loop combination in competition. His list of figure-skating firsts didn't end there: at the 1991 World Championships in Germany, the crowds saw Browning successfully complete the trio of the first triple axel-triple toe-loop; triple flip-triple toe loop; and triple salchow-triple loop.

Along the way to the 1992 Albertville Olympics, Browning won six major national and international competitions. Unfortunately, as in Calgary, Browning missed the Olympic podium in Albertville. He went on to instead take gold in the Canadian Championships, World Championships and Skate Canada before trying his skill at his last Olympics in 1994. Browning carried the Canadian flag in the opening ceremonies at Lillehammer, but did not come home with a medal, finishing fifth, and famously apologizing to Canadians afterward with a heartfelt "sorry."

Browning retired from amateur competition after the 1994 Olympics, but did not walk away without awards and honours aplenty in recognition of his amateur career. He was the first Canadian to top three consecutive World Championships, was the winner of a Lou Marsh Trophy and two Lionel Conacher Awards (his first marking the debut of a figure skater being honoured with this award) and was bestowed with an Order of Canada.

His professional career has been no less successful than his time in the amateurs, and the "Kid from Caroline" has enjoyed being part of the Stars on Ice Tour in both Canada and the U.S., as well as three-time World Professional Champion, four-time Canadian Professional Champion and two-time U.S. Professional Champion. Browning's accolades have continued to pour in, making him a celebrity recognized the world over. The International Skating Union awarded him the highest honour in the skating world, the Jacques Favart Trophy, in 1998, marking the first time a Canadian had ever received the award. And in 1999, Browning was recognized on *Jeopardy!* as the answer to a question. He also became the first Canadian athlete to be featured on the front of an American cereal box—Special K.

A member of Canada's Sports Hall of Fame and Skate Canada Hall of Fame, as well as an inductee of Canada's Walk of Fame, Browning is still active in figure skating, 21 years after his famous quadruple jump in 1988. And judging by his achievements, he should have no trouble being remembered by Canadians for many generations to come.

Elvis Stojko

Known around the world as another of Canada's most famous figure skaters, Elvis Stojko deserves all the attention he gets. Unlike many Canadian athletes who started their childhood years playing hockey and found their true calling in another sport later on, Newmarket, Ontario-born Stojko knew from a very young age that he was destined to figure skate. Beginning to skate at age four and winning his first trophy when he was six, his rise to the upper echelons of the amateur figure-skating ranks was sure and steady, and in 1991 at the World Championships he became the first person to land a quadruple double-jump combination.

Stojko made his first appearance at the Olympics in 1992 in Albertville, but did not make the podium. In many of his major competitions, he placed directly behind his fellow high-ranking countryman Kurt Browning, proving to the world Stojko's skill on the ice.

Determined to place at his next Olympic Games, Stojko accomplished his goal, winning a silver medal in 1994 at Lillehammer. He achieved yet another first in 1997 at the Grand Prix in Hamilton, Ontario, when he landed a quadruple-triple combination in his free skate. Stojko won the event with a routine full of his signature martial-art-inspired moves, skating to the soundtrack of the movie Dragon Heart.

A year later Stojko travelled to the Nagano Olympic Games, heavily favoured to win a gold medal. It was not to be. Suffering from a nagging groin injury and the flu, Stojko failed to complete his planned quadruple-triple jump in the free skate and appeared crippled with pain after his performance in the long program. Stojko did, however, come through with another Olympic silver medal and was so gripped with pain afterward that he hobbled up to the podium wearing sneakers instead of the figure skates traditionally worn. Overcome with emotion in a post-Olympics interview, Stojko broke down in tears when he learned people called him "gutsy" and "full of courage" for his showing in Nagano.

Stojko decided to turn professional in 2002 after the Salt Lake City Olympics and only skated for four more years until retiring in 2006 with a gala performance at the Mariposa Skating Club in Barrie, Ontario, where he trained for most of his amateur career. In his retirement speech, he thanked many, including Canada and his fans, saying, "To the wonderful fans, I love all of you and I hate to say it but…Elvis…will be leaving the building." Soon after, Stojko moved to Guadalajara, Mexico, leaving the spotlight behind, where he eventually became coach to Mexican figure skater Humberto Contreras.

Stojko started to make headlines again in 2008 when he came out as opposed to the Beijing Olympics, saying Canadian athletes should "make a stand" for human rights and think twice about heading to the Summer Games, and that if he were still a competing athlete, he would consider boycotting Beijing 2008. Also, as recently as 2009, it was reported that Stojko was preparing to launch a professional touring career:

I'm getting myself back in shape and getting on the ice. It's been really nice, a purity of skating, a change in the way I approach it and the style—a new vision. I had to end it completely because if you sort of take a half-step away, everyone still wants a piece of you because you're half in, half out. So that's why I ended it, I didn't know if I was going to come back. I'm back now.

Record-breaking Fact

The first figure skaters from Canada to claim a medal in ice dancing at the Olympic Winter Games were Tracy Wilson and Robert McCall. The pair won bronze before a hometown crowd at the 1988 Games in Calgary, Alberta.

Barbara Ann Scott

Known as "Canada's Sweetheart" and "Canada's Queen of the Ice Lanes," many Canadians of the new millennium still might find Barbara Ann Scott's likeness in their attics—in the form of dolls, stuffed toys and replicated Barbara Ann Scott figure skates. Some Canadian women might even bear Scott's first and second names, the result of the craze in Canada that saw each and every Canuck fall in love with Barbara Ann.

Born in Ottawa, Ontario, in 1928, Scott won her first figure-skating championship at the age of 11 and two years later became the first female skater to land the double Lutz in competition. Experiencing true glory following the end of World War II, Scott had Canada watching her with enthusiasm and excitement as she lifted her country's spirits after so much loss. Canada cheered for her when she became the first North American to win the European and World Championships in 1947, and again at the St. Mortiz Olympics in 1948 when Scott became the first Canadian figure skater to win a gold medal at the Winter Games. In that same year, she was also the World, European, North American and Canadian female figure-skating champion. In combination, these five wins made Scott the only person to ever become champion in each competition in the same year.

A darling of the media, Scott was never shy about sharing her experiences on the ice, and after her gold-medal win in St. Moritz, Switzerland, she revealed that she had skated on less-than-perfect ice on the outdoor rink where she claimed her victory:

> *The first day, we went to the rink to do school figures and they sent us home because the ice was too soft. I remember so well the day of the free skating. They played two hockey games that morning. I went onto the ice with my coach to see where the holes and ruts were so I wouldn't do a jump where there was a hole.*

It was Canada's men's hockey team who had taken to the ice before Scott, in a game they won. The ice surface, however, left Scott unperturbed, as she later said, "When you have to skate outside in the elements, you tend not to worry about the small stuff."

It was this positive attitude and outlook that caused Canada's Barbara Ann frenzy in the late 1940s and early 1950s, years that were full of international newspapers articles about Scott and tributes in the form of dolls, skates and stuffed toys. Scott was inducted into the Canadian

Olympic Hall of Fame in 1948, Canada's Sports
Hall of Fame in 1955, the Ottawa Sports Hall of
Fame in 1966, the American Hall of Fame in 1980,
the Canadian Figure Skating Hall of Fame in
1991 and the International Hall of Fame in 1997.
She also has a place on Canada's Walk of Fame, is
an officer of the Order of Canada and was
appointed to the Order of Ontario in 2009. "I'm
hanging in there, for an old lady," Scott has said.

Montgomery Wilson

Born in Toronto in 1909, Montgomery "Bud"
Wilson secured Canada's reputation as a country
to beat in the world of figure skating. Wilson
holds the record for the most Canadian titles won
by any skater, winning nine Canadian
Championships in singles between 1929 and
1939 and many more silver and bronze medals
on the national and international stage. The
length of time he reigned as Canadian champion
was not equalled until Brian Orser matched him
in the 1980s.

Wilson was also the first Canadian to place in
the top three at the World Championships.
Consequently, he was the first Canadian man to
win a medal at the 1932 Worlds with a silver in
Montréal. Wilson also became the first North

American man and first Canadian to place in the top three in figure skating at an Olympics with the bronze medal at the 1932 Lake Placid Games.

Competing in the singles, pairs and fours events throughout the course of his career, Wilson's total amount of figure-skating titles was unprecedented at the time of his fame and still remains so in the new millennium. He was inducted into the World Figure Skating Hall of Fame in 1976, into the Canadian Figure Skating Hall of Fame in 1990 and the Canadian Olympic Hall of Fame in 2007. Wilson died in 1964 after spending his post-skating years teaching at the Boston Skating Club and at Michigan State University.

Record-breaking Fact

At the 1948 Olympics in St. Moritz, Switzerland, Canada's Suzanne Morrow and partner Wallace Diestelmeyer became the first pair to perform the fabled death spiral in Olympic figure-skating competition. Their daring move catapulted them to a bronze-medal finish. The death spiral is performed when one partner (usually the man) braces himself with one skate in the ice and is used as a pivot while his partner extends her body, circling around him with one blade touching the ice.

Bobsleigh

Vic Emery

Vic Emery saw the bobsleigh event for the first time at the 1956 Cortina d'Ampezzo Olympics and immediately fell in love with the sport. Although many Canadians had never even heard of the bobsled and Canada did not have a track for athletes to practice on, Emery knew he had to get a team together for the 1964 Olympics in Innsbruck, Austria. He found willing partners in his brother John and friends Peter Kirby and Doug Anakin.

Virtual unknowns going into the 1964 Games, the Canadians surprised the world when they won the bobsled event by more than a second faster than their closest opponents. Canada did not win another bobsleigh medal until 1998 when Pierre Lueders and Dave MacEachern won gold in the two-man event.

Skiing

Nancy Greene

Named Canada's top female athlete of the 20th century by the Canadian Press and Broadcast News, alpine skier Nancy Greene has long been the pride of Canada in the sport of skiing. Born in 1943 in Ottawa, Greene and her family moved to Rossland, BC, where she started her skiing career when she was three years old. As she grew up, Greene moved quickly through the ranks in junior, national and U.S. championships, and in 1967 edged out the European competition to win the overall World Cup with top spots in four giant slaloms, two slaloms and one downhill. Green won the overall World Cup again in 1968, proving she was more than ready for the Winter Olympics in Grenoble that year. Building on her 13 World Cup event victories—the most ever won by a Canadian—in competition at Grenoble she won the gold medal in giant slalom by one of the largest margins in Olympic history. After her win, Greene said, "I think perhaps it was my greatest race ever." She also took home a silver medal in slalom.

For her efforts on the slopes and in Canadian sport, she was awarded the Bobbie Rosenfeld Award in 1967 and 1968 as the top female athlete in Canada, but decided to end her career while at the height of her success, retiring soon after Grenoble. Greene went on to make significant contributions to Canada's skiing community and was a key person in the development of the Whistler-Blackcomb Resort in Whistler, BC, and the Sun Peaks Resort north of Kamloops, BC. She has also played an integral role in bringing worldwide attention to Canada's ski-tourism industry. As a result of her many life achievements, Greene's honours include acting as the namesake for the Nancy Greene Provincial Park and Nancy Greene Lake in BC, a star on Canada's Walk of Fame, a place in Canada's Sports Hall of Fame and an Order of Canada. Green was also named to the Canadian Senate in 2008 by Prime Minister Stephen Harper.

Record-breaking Fact

Dave Irwin, Dave Murray, Steve Podborski, Jim Hunter and Ken Read make up Canada's famous alpine-skiing quintet, the Crazy Canucks. During the 1970s and '80s, these five men took the glory away from long-dominant European skiing champions. Known for their speed and the daring way they approached the sport, the Crazy Canucks had Canadians glued to their televisions. Read, Podborski, Hunter and Murray retired from the sport in the early 1980s, but not without a slew of accolades. Read was the first Canadian and North American male to win a World Cup downhill event, as well as the first non-European to win both the notorious Austrian Hahnenkamm and Swiss Lauberhorn races. Podborski took home a bronze medal at the 1980 Lake Placid Olympics and was the first North

American to win the World Cup season title in the downhill event. Hunter was the first Canadian male skier to win a World Championship bronze, and he also claimed a bronze medal at the 1972 Olympics in Sapporo, Japan. Read and Podborski continued to work in skiing after retirement and Hunter became a motivational speaker. Sadly, Murray died of skin cancer in 1990 and Irwin suffered a near-fatal crash while skiing in 2001, losing all of his memory as a result. However, the achievements of the Crazy Canucks have never been forgotten, and each lives on in Canadian sports history.

Record-breaking Fact

On one of the most difficult downhill runs in Olympic history, Kerrin Lee-Gartner of Trail, BC, performed flawlessly on the slopes in 1992 in Albertville. She beat out an extremely deep field of skiers to take the gold medal in women's downhill skiing, becoming the first Canadian ski racer to win an Olympic gold medal in the downhill event.

Bobbie Rosenfeld Award

Each year the Canadian Press awards the Bobbie Rosenfeld Trophy to Canada's top female athlete. The honour is named after the late Canadian track and field star Bobbie Rosenfeld.

Bobbie Rosenfeld Award Winners		
Year	Athlete	Sport
2008	Chantal Petitclerc	Wheelchair Racing
2007	Hayley Wickenheiser	Hockey
2006	Cindy Klassen	Speed Skating
2005	Cindy Klassen	Speed Skating
2004	Lori-Ann Muenzer	Cycling
2003	Perdita Felicien	Track and Field
2002	Catriona Le May-Doan	Speed Skating
2001	Catriona Le May-Doan	Speed Skating
2000	Lorie Kane	Golf
1999	Nancy Greene (Athlete of the Century)	Skiing
1998	Catriona Le May-Doan	Speed Skating
1997	Lorie Kane	Golf
1996	Alison Sydor	Cycling
1995	Susan Auch	Speed Skating
1994	Myriam Bedard	Biathlon
1993	Kate Pace	Skiing
1992	Silken Laumann	Rowing
1991	Silken Laumann	Rowing
1990	Helen Kelesi	Tennis
1989	Helen Kelesi	Tennis
1988	Carolyn Waldo	Synchronized Swimming
1987	Carolyn Waldo	Synchronized Swimming

Bobbie Rosenfeld cont.

Year	Athlete	Sport
1986	Laurie Graham	Skiing
1985	Carling Bassett	Tennis
1984	Sylvie Bernier	Diving
1983	Carling Bassett	Tennis
1982	Gerry Sorenson	Skiing
1981	Tracey Wainman	Figure Skating
1980	Sandra Post	Golf
1979	Sandra Post	Golf
1978	Diane Jones-Konihowski	Pentathlon
1977	Cindy Nicholas	Swimming
1976	Kathy Kreiner	Skiing
1975	Nancy Garapick	Swimming
1974	Wendy Cook	Swimming
1973	Karen Magnussen	Figure Skating
1972	Jocelyn Bourassa	Golf
1971	Debbie Van Kiekebelt and Debbie Brill	Pentathlon and High Jump
1970	Beverley Boys	Diving
1969	Beverley Boys	Diving
1968	Nancy Greene	Skiing
1967	Nancy Greene	Skiing
1966	Elaine Tanner	Swimming
1965	Petra Burka	Figure Skating
1964	Petra Burka	Figure Skating
1963	Marlene Streit	Golf
1962	Mary Stewart	Swimming
1961	Mary Stewart	Swimming
1960	Anne Heggtveit	Skiing
1959	Anne Heggtveit	Skiing
1958	Lucile Wheeler	Skiing

Bobbie Rosenfeld cont.

Year	Athlete	Sport
1957	Marlene Streit	Golf
1956	Marlene Streit	Golf
1955	Marilyn Bell	Swimming
1954	Marilyn Bell	Swimming
1953	Marlene Streit	Golf
1952	Marlene Streit	Golf
1951	No award given	—
1950	Bobbie Rosenfeld (Athlete of the Half Century)	Track and Field
1949	Irene Strong	Swimming
1948	Barbara Ann Scott	Figure Skating
1947	Barbara Ann Scott	Figure Skating
1946	Barbara Ann Scott	Figure Skating
1945	No award because of World War II	—
1944	No award because of World War II	—
1943	No award because of World War II	—
1942	No award because of World War II	—
1941	Mary Rose Thacker	Figure Skating
1940	Dorothy Walton	Badminton
1939	Mary Rose Thacker	Figure Skating
1938	Noel MacDonald	Basketball
1937	Robina Higgins	Track and Field
1936	Betty Taylor	Track and Field
1935	Aileen Meagher	Track and Field
1934	Pyhllis Dewar	Swimming
1933	Ada Mackenzie	Golf

Chapter Two

Olympic Recollections

1904 Olympic Games in St. Louis

Lacrosse is the only Olympic sport to which Canada can claim complete dominance. Included in the Olympic calendar for just two Games, in 1904 and 1908, Canadian teams won the gold medal both times. In 1908 when Canada defeated Great Britain to win the gold medal, no other teams were part of the event.

1920 Olympic Games in Antwerp

It has gone down in the history books that Canada's first gold medal in Olympic ice hockey came at the first-ever Winter Olympics in Chamonix, France, in 1924. Canada, however, technically won its inaugural Olympic-hockey gold at the 1920 Olympics in Belgium. This was the year and location that featured the normally scheduled Summer Games as well as the debut of the Winter Olympics. Belgian spectators had the rare experience of watching both summer-event athletes as well as hockey players and figure skaters compete for podium finishes

Canada's hockey entry was the Winnipeg Falcons team that had just finished an incredible season in the Senior Amateur Hockey League, winning the 1920 Allan Cup Championship. Because of the team's superior hockey skills, the International Olympic Committee (IOC) asked them to join their fellow Canadian athletes at the 1920 Olympics in Antwerp, Belgium. With dreams of Olympic gold in their heads, the Canadian men's hockey team bulldozed their way through the competition, beating the U.S., Sweden and Czechoslovakia by a combined score of 28–1.

Along with their medals, the Falcons received an official piece of paper stating they had won the hockey gold medal of the first official Winter Olympic Games. Unfortunately, the IOC later repealed their decision to name the 1920 Belgium Olympics the first Winter Games and instead gave that distinction to the 1924 Chamonix Olympics. The Canadian hockey team also won the gold medal at the 1924 Games and were officially given the recognition as the first team to win Olympic hockey gold—again.

1932 Olympic Games in Lake Placid

Canada won its first non-hockey medal at the 1932 Winter Games in Lake Placid. Because of the city's relative proximity to Canada, Canadian athletes could afford the short journey across the U.S. border. Apart from winning hockey gold in 1932, Canadians also took home one silver and five bronze in figure-skating and speed-skating events.

Canada also took part in dog-sled racing at Lake Placid. Although dog-sledding was never made an official Olympic event, it was featured as a demonstration sport at the 1932 Games. Canada dominated the field, taking first, second and third place, with Emile St. Goddard of Manitoba claiming the gold medal.

1936 Olympic Games in Garmisch-Partenkirchen

Canada sent 45-year-old Edwina Chamier to the 1936 Winter Games in Garmisch-Partenkirchen, Germany, to compete in the alpine skiing combined event. At 45 years and 318 days old at the time, she is the oldest Olympic competitor of the 20th century.

1952 Olympic Games in Oslo

In 1952, the Edmonton Mercurys travelled to Oslo, Norway, as Canada's Olympic hockey team. In five previous Winter Games, Canada won four gold medals and one silver, but by the time the 1952 Olympics rolled around, the rest of the world had caught up in skill level and Canada would no longer have an easy ride to the gold. The Mercurys managed to claim first place, but it was the last time Canada saw the hockey gold medal in the 20th century. It wasn't until 50 years later in 2002 at the Salt Lake City Olympics that Canada took gold again, beating the U.S. 5–2.

1960 Olympic Games in Rome

While not a record Canada is proud of, the country's worst-ever showing at the Olympics was in 1960 in Rome. Canada took home only one medal, a silver in the men's eights rowing event. Great things were expected of Canadian sprinter Harry Jerome because he had tied the world record in the 100-metre at 10.0 seconds, but he was forced out in a semifinal race after sustaining a serious thigh injury.

1976 Olympic Games in Montréal

Canada became the first Olympic host nation to finish the Olympics without having won a gold medal. Canada didn't win a gold at the 1988 Winter Games in Calgary, either.

Record-breaking Fact

Not many athletes are able to train at the same time for two completely different sports, but Halifax, Nova Scotia native Sue Holloway is the first Canadian athlete to have competed in the Summer and Winter Olympics in the same year. At the 1976 Winter Olympics in Innsbruck, Austria, Holloway proudly represented her country in the cross-country relay race and then switched gears for the Summer Olympics in Montréal later that year to compete in the C-2 canoeing event. Despite her tenacity, she did not win any medals.

1980 Olympic Games in Moscow

When it was announced that the United States was boycotting the Moscow Games, Canada soon followed suit. The topic was hotly debated at the time because many athletes might have missed out on the one and only chance to ever qualify for the Olympics. Canada, however, more than made up for its absence, and at the 1984 Games in Los Angeles, had its best Olympic showing to date.

1984 Olympic Games in Los Angeles

Canada sent 436 athletes to Los Angeles, and when all was said and done, finished with 10 gold, 18 silver and 16 bronze for a best-ever grand total of 44 medals. The closest Canada has come to equalling this mark since was in 1996 in Atlanta when 307 athletes brought back 22 medals.

Record-breaking Fact

Canada became the first nation to win a gold medal in the sport of rhythmic gymnastics when Vancouver, BC's Lori Fung beat out the competition at the 1984 Olympics in Los Angeles.

1988 Olympic Games in Calgary

Prior to the 1988 Olympics in Calgary, the figure-skating world's attention was focused on the top two women in the sport, German Katarina Witt and American Debi Thomas. Ottawa native Elizabeth Manley was not seen as a possible gold-medal contender. Even her hometown newspaper the *Ottawa Citizen* had written her off as inconsistent and having no chance of matching the performances of the world's top athletes. Manley herself was simply hoping for a top-six finish, a medal being the ultimate prize.

In the first of the three-part figure-skating competition in Calgary, Manley, who was battling the flu, managed to finish in fourth place. She was still feeling the effects of her flu in the short program, but once out on the ice, Manley put on the performance of a lifetime, landing all her jumps and nailing all the technical requirements. Her short program moved her into third place, putting her into serious contention for the gold.

In her long program, Manley performed each element of her routine with flawless grace and each successful completion saw the crowd's cheers get louder. In her routine, she pulled off five triple jumps, and when she ended her program at centre ice, Manley put her hands to her face in disbelief at the performance she had just given. She finished first place in the long program and second place overall, earning a silver medal. Manley also placed second at the World Championships in 1988, and retired from amateur skating shortly afterward.

1994 Olympic Games in Lillehammer

Canada's hope for a women's figure-skating medal in the 1994 Lillehammer Olympics,

Montréal native Josée Chouinard took to the ice amid a flurry of controversy. In the lead-up to the 1994 Olympics, at a U.S. Figure Skating Championship practice session that year, U.S. skater Nancy Kerrigan was attacked by an unknown assailant. It was later discovered that American rival Tonya Harding had plotted the attack to remove Kerrigan from competition so Harding could take her place as the top U.S. women's figure-skating contender at the Lillehammer Olympics. Harding was supposed to be stripped of her Olympic athlete title because of the attack, but when the U.S. Olympic Committee tried to remove her from the American team, she threatened to sue and was allowed to participate.

Chouinard was scheduled to perform her free skate immediately after Harding in Norway, and the placement turned out to be an unlucky one. During Harding's performance, she stopped midway through and asked the judges if she could restart because of a broken skate lace. Harding was allowed to begin again after replacing her lace, but because she used up too much time with her start and restart, the next skater, Chouinard, was forced onto the ice prematurely without the chance for a brief warm-up. Chouinard fell three times and appeared shaky throughout, finishing with a performance that left Canada stunned and placed her ninth overall. Afterward, many Canadians speculated that Harding's antics had resulted in a rattled Chouinard, robbing her and Canada of the Olympic medal all had hoped for.

Record-breaking Fact

Myriam Bédard of Neufchâtel, Québec, won the gold medals in the 15-kilometre and 7.5-kilometre biathlons at the 1994 Olympics in Lillehammer, Norway—the first woman to win gold medals in two biathlon events in the same Winter Games.

Canadian Medals by Sport—Summer Olympics				
Sport	Gold	Silver	Bronze	Total
Diving	1	2	4	7
Swimming	7	13	19	39
Synchronized Swimming	3	4	1	8
Athletics	13	14	23	50
Basketball	0	1	0	1
Boxing	3	7	7	17
Canoe/Kayak	4	8	7	19
Cycling	1	5	5	11
Equestrian	1	1	2	4
Football	1	0	0	1
Golf	1	0	0	1
Gymnastics—Artistic	1	0	3	4
Gymnastics—Rhythmic	1	0	0	1
Judo	0	2	2	4
Lacrosse	2	0	0	2

Medals by Sport—Summer Olympics cont.

Sport	Gold	Silver	Bronze	Total
Rowing	8	13	10	31
Sailing	0	3	6	9
Shooting	4	3	2	9
Taekwondo	0	0	1	1
Tennis	1	0	0	1
Triathlon	1	0	0	1
Volleyball	0	0	1	1
Weightlifting	0	2	0	2
Wrestling	1	5	5	11
Total	54	83	98	235

Canadian Medals by Sport—Winter Olympics

Sport	Gold	Silver	Bronze	Total
Alpine Skiing	4	1	5	10
Biathlon	2	0	1	3
Bobsleigh	2	1	0	3
Cross-country Skiing	2	1	0	3
Curling	2	2	2	6
Figure Skating	3	7	10	20
Freestyle Skiing	2	2	2	6
Ice Hockey	8	5	2	15
Long-track Speed Skating	6	10	12	28
Luge	0	0	0	0
Nordic Combined	0	0	0	0
Skeleton	1	1	1	3
Ski Jumping	0	0	0	0
Snowboard	1	0	1	2
Short-track Speed Skating	5	8	7	20
Total	38	38	43	119

Canadian Medals by Olympics—Summer

Year	City	Gold	Silver	Bronze	Total
2008	Beijing (China)	3	9	6	18
2004	Athens (Greece)	3	6	3	12
2000	Sydney (Australia)	3	3	8	14
1996	Atlanta (U.S.)	3	11	8	22
1992	Barcelona (Spain)	7	4	7	18
1988	Seoul (South Korea)	3	2	5	10
1984	Los Angeles (U.S.)	10	18	16	44
1980	Moscow (Russia) Did not compete—boycott	—	—	—	—
1976	Montreal (Canada)	0	5	6	11
1972	Munich (Germany)	0	2	3	5
1968	Mexico City (Mexico)	1	3	1	5
1964	Tokyo (Japan)	1	2	1	4
1960	Rome (Italy)	0	1	0	1
1956	Melbourne (Australia)	2	1	3	6
1952	Helsinki (Finland)	1	2	0	3
1948	London (England)	0	1	2	3
1944	Games not held	—	—	—	—
1940	Games not held	—	—	—	—
1936	Berlin (Germany)	1	3	5	9
1932	Los Angeles (U.S.)	2	5	8	15
1928	Amsterdam (Holland)	4	4	7	15
1924	Paris (France)	0	3	1	4
1920	Antwerp (Belgium)	3	3	3	9
1916	Games not held	—	—	—	—
1912	Stockholm (Sweden)	3	2	3	8
1908	London (England)	3	3	10	16
1906	Athens (Greece) *	1	1	0	2
1904	St. Louis (U.S.)	4	1	1	6
1900	Paris (France)	1	0	1	2

Canadian Medals by Olympics—Summer cont.

Year	City	Gold	Silver	Bronze	Total
1896	Athens (Greece) Did not compete	—	—	—	—

*Intercalated Games that are not recognized by the IOC

Canadian Medals by Olympics—Winter

Year	City	Gold	Silver	Bronze	Total
2006	Turin (Italy)	7	10	7	24
2002	Salt Lake City (U.S.)	7	3	7	17
1998	Nagano (Japan)	6	5	4	15
1994	Lillehammer (Norway)	3	6	4	13
1992	Albertville (France)	2	3	2	7
1988	Calgary (Canada)	0	2	3	5
1984	Sarajevo (Yugoslavia)	2	1	1	4
1980	Lake Placid (U.S.)	0	1	1	2
1976	Innsbruck (Austria)	1	1	1	3
1972	Sapporo (Japan)	0	1	0	1
1968	Grenoble (France)	1	1	1	3
1964	Innsbruck (Austria)	1	0	2	3
1960	Squaw Valley (U.S.)	2	1	1	4
1956	Cortina d'Ampezzo (Italy)	0	1	2	3
1952	Oslo (Norway)	1	0	1	2
1948	St. Moritz (Switzerland)	2	0	1	3
1944	Games not held	—	—	—	—
1940	Games not held	—	—	—	—
1936	Garmisch-Partenkirchen (Germany)	0	1	0	1
1932	Lake Placid (U.S.)	1	1	5	7

Canadian Medals by Olympics—Winter cont.

Year	City	Gold	Silver	Bronze	Total
1928	St. Moritz (Switzerland)	1	0	0	1
1924	Chamonix (France)	1	0	0	1

Most Canadian Men's Olympic Medals

Career

5	Philip Edwards	Athletics	
		1928—4x400m Relay	Bronze
		1932—800m	Bronze
		1932—1500m	Bronze
		1932—4x400m Relay	Bronze
		1936—800m	Bronze
5	Marc Gagnon	Short-Track Speed Skating	
		1994—1000m	Bronze
		1998—5000m relay	Gold
		2002—500m	Gold
		2002—5000m Relay	Gold
		2002—1500m	Bronze

At one Games

3	Victor Davis	Swimming—1984	
		200m Breaststroke	Gold
		100m Breaststroke	Silver
		4x100m Medley Relay	Silver
3	Philip Edwards	Athletics—1932	
		1500m	Bronze
		4x400m Relay	Bronze
		800m	Bronze

Most Canadian Men's Olympic Medals cont.

At one Games

3	Marc Gagnon	Short-track Speed Skating—2002	
		500m	Gold
		5000m relay	Gold
		1500m	Bronze

Most Canadian Women's Olympic Medals

Career

6	Cindy Klassen	Long-track Speed Skating	
		2006—1500m	Gold
		2006—1000m	Silver
		2006—Team Pursuit	Silver
		2006—5000m	Bronze
		2006—3000m	Bronze
		2002—3000m	Bronze
4	Kathleen Heddle	Rowing	
		1992—Coxless Pairs	Gold
		1992—Eights	Gold
		1996—Double Sculls	Gold
		1996—Quadruple Sculls	Bronze
4	Marnie McBean	Rowing	
		1992—Coxless Pairs	Gold
		1992—Eights	Gold
		1996—Double Sculls	Gold
		1996—Quadruple Sculls	Bronze
4	Lesley Thompson	Rowing	
		1992—Eights	Gold
		1984—Coxed Fours	Silver
		1996—Eights	Silver
		2000—Eights	Bronze

Most Canadian Women's Olympic Medals cont.

At one Games

5	Cindy Klassen	Long-track Speed Skating—2006	
		1500m	Gold
		1000m	Silver
		Team Pursuit	Silver
		5000m	Bronze
		3000m	Bronze
3	Anne Ottenbrite	Swimming—1984	
		200m Breaststroke	Gold
		100m Breaststroke	Silver
		4x100m Medley Relay	Bronze
3	Elaine Tanner	Swimming—1968	
		100m Backstroke	Silver
		200m Backstroke	Silver
		4x100m Freestyle Relay	Bronze

Summer Olympics Medal List

GOLD

Year	Athlete	Event
2008	Eric Lamaze	Equestrian— Individual Jumping
	Carol Huynh	Freestyle Wrestling
	Kevin Light, Ben Rutledge, Andrew Byrnes, Jake Wezel, Malcolm Howard, Dominic Seiterle, Adam Kreek, Kyle Hamilton, Brian Price	Rowing—Eights
2004	Kyle Shewfelt	Gymnastics—Floor Exercise
	Lori-Ann Muenzer	Sprint Cycling
	Adam van Koeverden	500m Kayak Singles
2000	Daniel Nestor, Sebastien Lareau	Doubles Tennis

Summer Medal List cont.

GOLD

Year	Athlete	Event
2000	Simon Whitfield	Triathlon
	Daniel Igali	Freestyle Wrestling
1996	Donovan Bailey	100m Sprint
	Kathleen Heddle, Marnie McBean	Rowing—Double Sculls
	Donovan Bailey, Robert Esmie, Bruny Surin, Glenroy Gilbert	4x100m Relay
1992	Mark McKoy	110m Hurdles
	Kathleen Heddle, Marnie McBean	Rowing—Coxless Pairs
	Kirsten Barnes, Jessica Monroe, Brenda Taylor, Kay Worthington	Rowing—Coxless Fours
	Lesley Thompson, Kathleen Heddle, Marnie McBean, Kirsten Barnes, Megan Delehanty, Jessica Monroe, Brenda Taylor, Kay Worthington, Shannon Crawford	Rowing—Eights
	Derek Porter, Michael Rascher, Bruce Robertson, Andy Crosby, Mike Forgeron, Robert Marland, Darren Barber, Terry Paul, John Wallace	Rowing—Eights
	Mark Tewksbury	100m Backstroke Swim
	Sylvie Frechette	Synchronized Swimming—Solo
1988	Lennox Lewis	Super Heavyweight Boxing
	Carolyn Waldo	Synchronized Swimming—Solo
	Ben Johnson*	100m Sprint
1984	Alex Baumann	200m Individual Medley Swim

*(Medal stripped because of doping)

Summer Medal List cont.

GOLD

Year	Athlete	Event
1984	Alex Baumann	400m Individual Medley Swim
	Linda Thom	Sport Pistol
	Victor Davis	200m Breaststroke Swim
	Anne Ottenbrite	200m Breaststroke Swim
	Pat Turner, Brian McMahon, Kevin Neufeld, Mark Evans, Grant Main, Pault Steele, Mike Evans, Dean Crawford, Blair Horn	Rowing—Coxed Heavy Eights
	Sylvie Bernier	3m Springboard Diving
	Lori Fung	Rhythmic Gymnastics
	Larry Cain	500m Single Canoe
	Hugh Fisher, Alwyn Morris	1000m Kayak Pairs
1980	Did not attend due to boycott	—
1976	No gold medals	—
1972	No gold medals	—
1968	Jim Elder, Jim Day, Tom Gayford	Equestrian Prix des Nations
1964	Roger Jackson, George Hungerford	Rowing—Coxless Pairs
1960	No gold medals	
1956	Don Arnold, Walter D'Hondt, Lorne Loomer, Archie McKinnon	Rowing—Coxless Fours
	Gerry Ouelette	Smallbore Shooting—Smallbore-prone
1952	George Genereux	Trap Shooting

Summer Medal List cont.

GOLD

Year	Athlete	Event
1946	No Olympics due to World War II	—
1940	No Olympics due to World War II	—
1936	Frank Amyot	Canoeing—1000m Singles
1932	Lefty Gwynne	Bantamweight Boxing
	Duncan McNaughton	High Jump
1928	Percy Williams	100m Sprint
	Percy Williams	200m Sprint
	Bobbie Rosenfeld, Ethel Smith, Florence Bell, Myrtle Cook	4x100m Relay
	Ethel Catherwood	High Jump
1920	Bert Schneider	Welterweight Boxing
	Earl Thomson	100m Hurdles
1916	No Olympics due to World War I	—
1912	George Goulding	10,000m Walk
	George Hodgson	1500m Swim
	George Hodgson	400m Swim
1908	Bobby Kerr	200m Sprint
	Walter Ewing	Trap Shooting
	The All-Canadas: Patrick Brennan, John Broderick, George Campbell, Angus Dillion, Frank Dixon, Richard Duckett, J. Fyon, Tommy Gorman, Ernest Hamilton, Henry Hoobin, Albert Mara, Clarence McKerrow, David MacLeod, George Rennie, Alex Turnbull	Lacrosse
1906	William Sherring	Marathon
1904	Etienne Desmarteau	Weight Toss
	Galt Football Club: George Ducker, John Fraser, John Gourley, Alex Hall, Albert Johnson, Robert Lane, Ernest Linton, Gordon McDonald, Fred Steep, Tom Taylor, William Twaits	Soccer

Summer Medal List cont.

GOLD

Year	Athlete	Event
1904	George S. Lyon	Golf
	Winnipeg Shamrocks: Eli Blanchard, V. Brennaugh, George Bretz, William Burns, George Cattanach, George Cloutier, Sandy Cowan, Jack Flett, Benjamin Jamieson, Hilliard Laidlaw, H.Lyle, William Orris, L.H. Pentland	Lacrosse
1900	George Orton	Steeplechase—3000m

SILVER

Year	Athlete	Event
2008	Karen Cockburn	Trampoline
	David Calder, Scott Frandsen	Rowing—Coxless Pairs
	Mac Cone, Jill Henselwood, Eric Lamaze, Ian Millar	Equestrian—Team Jumping
	Simon Whitfield	Triathlon
	Jason Burnett	Trampoline
	Alexandre Despatie	Diving—3m Springboard
	Emilie Heymans	Diving—10m Platform
	Karine Sergerie	Tae Kwon Do
	Adam van Koeverden	Canoeing—K-1 500m
2004	Karen Cockburn	Trampoline
	Cameron Baerg, Thomas Herschmiller, Jake Wetzel, Barney Williams	Rowing—Coxless Fours
	Tonya Verbeek	Freestyle Wrestling
	Alexandre Despatie	Diving—3m Springboard

Summer Medal List cont.

SILVER

Year	Athlete	Event
2004	Marrie-Helene Premont	Mountain Biking
	Ross MacDonald, Mike Wolfs	Yachting—Star
2000	Caroline Brunet	Canoeing—K-1 500m
	Anne Montminy, Emile Heymans	Diving—Synchronized, 10m Platform
	Nicolas Gill	Judo
1996	David Defiagbon	Heavyweight Boxing
	Caroline Brunet	Canoeing—K-1 500m
	Brian Walton	Cycling—Individual Points Race
	Alison Sydor	Cycling—Cross Country
	David Boyes, Gavin Hassett, Jeffrey Lay, Brian Parker	Rowing—Coxless Fours
	Alison Korn, Theresa Luke, Maria Maunder, Heather McDermid, Jessica Monroe, Emma Robinson, Lesley Thompson, Tosha Tsang, Anna Van der Kamp	Rowing—Eights
	Silken Laumann	Rowing—Single Sculls
	Derek Porter	Rowing—Single Sculls
	Marianne Limpert	200m Individual Medley Swim
	Lisa Alexander, Janice Bremner, Karen Clark, Karen Fontenyne, Sylvie Frechette, Valerie Marchand, Christine Larsen, Cari Read, Erin Woodley	Synchronized Swimming—Team
	Gia Sissauori	Freestyle Wrestling

Summer Medal List cont.

SILVER

Year	Athlete	Event
1992	Mark Leduc	Light Welterweight Boxing
	Penny Vilagos, Vicky Vilagos	Synchronized Swimming—Duet
	Guillaume Leblanc	20km Walk
	Jeff Thue	Freestyle Wrestling
1988	Egerton Marcus	Middleweight Boxing
	Mark Tewksbury, Victor Davis, Tom Ponting, Sandy Goss	4x100m Medley Swim
1984	Victor Davis	100m Breaststroke Swim
	Steve Bauer	Cycling—190km Road Race
	Curt Harnett	Cycling—1000m Time Trial
	Willie De Wit	Heavyweight Boxing
	Shawn O'Sullivan	Light Middleweight Boxing
	Alexandra Barre, Sue Halloway	Canoeing—K-2 500m
	Larry Cain	Canoeing—C-1 1000m
	Barbara Armburst, Marilyn Brian, Angela Schneider, Lesley Thompson, Jane Tregunno	Rowing— Coxed Fours
	Betty Craig, Tricia Smith	Rowing—Coxless Pairs
	Victor Davis, Sandy Goss, Tom Ponting, Mike West	4x100m Medley Swim
	Anne Ottenbrite	100m Breaststroke Swim

Summer Medal List cont.

SILVER

Year	Athlete	Event
1984	Carolyn Waldo	Synchronized Swimming— Solo
	Sharon Hambrook, Kelly Kryczka	Synchronized Swimming— Duet
	Angela Bailey, France Gareau, Marita Payne, Angella Taylor	4x100m Relay
	Charmaine Crooks, Molly Killingbeck, Marita Payne, Jillian Richardson	4x400m Relay
	Jacques Demers	Weightlifting
	Bob Molle	Freestyle Wrestling
	Evert Bastet, Terry McLaughlin	Yachting—Flying Dutchman
1976	Greg Joy	High Jump
	John Wood	Canoeing—C-1 500m
	Michel Vaillancourt	Equestrian—Grand Prix Jumping
	Cheryl Gibson	400m Individual Medley Swim
	Clay Evans, Gary MacDonald, Stephen Pickell, Graham Smith	4x100 Medley Relay Swim
1972	Leslie Cliff	400m Individual Medley Swim
	Bruce Robertson	100m Butterfly Swim
1968	Ralph Hutton	400m Freestyle Swim
	Elaine Tanner	100m Backstroke Swim
	Elaine Tanner	200m Backstroke Swim

Summer Medal List cont.

SILVER

Year	Athlete	Event
1964	Bill Crothers	800m Run
	Doug Rogers	Judo
1960	Donald Arnold, Walter D'Hondt, Nelson Kuhn, John Lecky, David Anderson, William McKerlich, Archie MacKinnon, Glen Mervyn, Sohen Biln	Rowing—Eights
1956	David Helliwell, Phillip Kueber, Richard McClure, Douglas McDonald, William McKerlich, Carleton Ogawa, Donald Pretty, Lawrence West, Robert Wilson	Rowing—Eights
1952	Doug Hawgood, Ken Lane	Canoeing—C-2 10,000m
	Gerald Gratton	Weightlifting
1948	Doug Bennett	Canoeing—1000m Singles
1946	No Olympics due to World War II	—
1940	No Olympics due to World War II	—
1936	Gord Aitchison, Ian Allison, Art Chapman, Charles Chapman, Edward Dawson, Irving Meretsky, Robert Osborne, Doug Peden, James Stewart, Malcolm Wiseman	Basketball
	Harvey Charters, Frank Saker	Canoeing—10,000m Doubles
	John Loaring	400m Hurdles
1932	Hilda Strike	100m Sprint
	Mary Frizzell, Mildred Frizzell, Lillian Palmer, Hilda Strike	4x100m Relay
	Alex Wilson	800m Run
	Dan MacDonald	Freestyle Wrestling
	Earnest Cribb, Peter Gordon, Georges Gyles, Harry Jones, Ronald Maitland, Hubert Wallace	Yachting—Team Eights

Summer Medal List cont.

SILVER

Year	Athlete	Event
1928	Jack Guest, Joe Wright Jr.	Rowing—Double Sculls
	Fanny Rosenfeld	100m Sprint
	Jim Ball	400m Run
	Donald Stockton	Freestyle Wrestling
1924	William Wood, Colin Finlayson, George McKay, Archie Black	Rowing—Coxless Fours
	Arthur Bell, Ivor Campbell, Robert Hunter, William Langford, Harold Little, John Smith, Warren Snyder, Norm Taylor, William Wallace	Rowing—Eights
	William Barnes, Georges Beattie, John Black, James Montgomery, Sam Newton, Sam Vance	Clay Pigeon—Team
1920	Charles Graham	Bantamweight Boxing
	Georges Prud'Homme	Middleweight Boxing
	George Vernot	1500m Swim
1916	No Olympics due to World War I	—
1912	Cal Bricker	Running Long Jump
	Duncan Gillis	Hammer Throw
1908	Garfield McDonald	Hop, Step and Jump (Triple Jump today)
	Con Walsh	Hammer Throw
	George Beattie	Clay Pigeon Shooting
	George Beattie, Walter Ewing, Mylie Fletcher, D. McMackon, George Vivian, A.W. Westover	Clay Pigeon—Team
1906	Donald Linden	1500m Walk
1904	A. Bailey, Phil Boyd, Thomas Loudon, Donald McKenzie, George Reiffenstein, W. Rice, George Strange, William Wadsworth	Rowing—Eights

Summer Medal List cont.

BRONZE

Year	Athlete	Event
2008	Tonya Verbeek	Freestyle Wrestling
	Ryan Cochrane	1500m Freestyle Swim
	Tracy Cameron, Melanie Kok	Rowing—Double Sculls
	Iain Brambell, Liam Parsons, Jon Beare, Mike Lewis	Rowing—Coxless Fours
	Priscilla Lopes-Schliep	100m Hurdles
	Thomas Hall	Canoeing—C-1 1000m
2004	Blythe Hartley, Emilie Heymans	Diving—Synchronized 10m
	Caroline Brunet	Canoeing—K-1 500m
	Adam van Koeverden	Canoeing—K-1 1000m
2000	Anne Montminy	Diving—10m Platform
	Curtis Myden	400m Individual Medley Swim
	Lyne Beaumont, Claire Dias, Erin Chan, Jessica Chase, Catherine Garceau, Fanny Leto, Kristin Normand, Jacinthe Taillon, Reidun Tathamurneau	Synchronized Swimming—Team
	Mathieu Turgeon	Trampoline
	Karen Cockburn	Trampoline
	Steve Giles	Canoeing—C-1 1000m
	Buffy Alexander, Laryssa Biesenthal, Heather Davis, Alison Korn, Theresa Luke, Heather McDermid, Emma Robinson, Lesley Thompson, Dorota Urbaniak	Rowing—Coxed Eights

Summer Medal List cont.

BRONZE

Year	Athlete	Event
2000	Dominque Bosshart	Tae Kwon Do
1996	Clara Hughes	Cycling—Road Race
	Clara Hughes	Cycling—Individual Time Trial
	Curtis Myden	400m Individual Medley Swim
	Curtis Myden	200m Individual Medley Swim
	John Child, Mark Hesse	Beach Volleyball
	Curt Harnett	Cycling—Sprint
	Marnie McBean, Kathleen Heddle, Laryssa Biesenthal, Diane O'Grady	Rowing—Fours Sculls
	Annie Pelletier	Diving—3m Springboard
1992	Chris Johnson	Middleweight Boxing
	Curt Hartnett	Cycling—Individual Sprint
	Nicolas Gill	Judo
	Silken Laumann	Rowing—Single Sculls
	Mark Tewksbury, Jon Cleveland, Marcel Gery, Stephen Clarke	4x100m Medley Relay Swim
	Angela Chalmers	3000m Run
	Ross MacDonald, Eric Jesperson	Yachting—Star
1988	Dave Steen	Decathlon
	Raymond Downey	Light Middleweight Boxing
	Cynthia Ishoy, Eva-Marie Pracht, Gina Smith, Ashley Nicoll	Equestrian—Team Dressage
	Lori Melien, Allison Higson, Jane Kerr, Andrea Nugent	4x100m Medley Relay Swim

Summer Medal List cont.

BRONZE

Year	Athlete	Event
1988	Frank McLaughlin, John Millen	Yachting—Flying Dutchman
1984	Reema Abdo, Anne Ottenbrite, Michelle MacPherson, Pam Rai	4x100 Medley Relay Swim
	Cameron Henning	200m Backstroke Swim
	Mike West	100m Backstroke Swim
	Daniele Laumann, Silken Laumann	Rowing—Double Sculls
	Ben Johnson	100m Sprint
	Ben Johnson, Tony Sharpe, Desai Williams, Sterling Hinds	4x100m Relay
	Bob Mills	Rowing—Single Sculls
	Bruce Ford, Phil Monckton, Mike Hughes, Doug Hamilton	Rowing—Coxless Fours Sculls
	Hugh Fisher, Alwyn Morris	Canoeing—K-2 500m
	Mark Berger	Judo
	Lynn Williams	3000m Run
	Dale Walters	Bantamweight Boxing
	Alexandra Barre, Sue Halloway, Lucie Guay, Barb Olmstead	Canoeing—K-4 500m
	Chris Rinke	Freestyle Wrestling
	Terry Neilson	Yachting—Finn
	Hans Fogh, Steve Calder, John Kerr	Yachting—Soling
1980	Did not attend due to boycott	—
1976	Nancy Garapick	100m Backstroke Swim

Summer Medal List cont.

BRONZE

Year	Athlete	Event
1976	Nancy Garapick	200m Backstroke Swim
	Shannon Smith	400m Freestyle Swim
	Becky Smith	400m Individual Medley Swim
	Gail Amundrud, Barbara Clark, Anne Jardin, Becky Smith	4x100 Freestyle Relay Swim
	Robin Corsiglia, Wendy Hogg, Anne Jardin, Susan Sloan	4x100 Medley Relay Swim
1972	Donna Gurr	100m Backstroke Swim
	Paul Cote, John Ekels, David Miller	Yachting—Soling
1968	Erik Fish, Bob Kasting, Bill Mahony, Bruce Robertson	4x100m Medley Relay Swim
1964	Harry Jerome	100m Sprint
1956	Gil Boa	Smallbore Shooting— Smallbore-prone
	Irene MacDonald	Diving—3m Springboard
	John Runble, Brian Herbinson, Jim Elder	Equestrian— Three-day Event
1948	Viola Myers, Nancy McKay, Dianne Foster, Patricia Jones	4x100m Relay
	Norm Lane	Canoeing—C-1 10,000m
1946	No Olympics due to World War II	—
1940	No Olympics due to World War II	—
1936	Phil Edwards	800m Run
	Betty Taylor	80m Hurdles

Summer Medal List cont.

BRONZE

Year	Athlete	Event
1936	Dorothy Brookshaw, Jeannette Dolson, Hilda Cameron, Aileen Meagher	4x100m Relay
	Joe Schleimer	Freestyle Wrestling
	Frank Saker, Harvey Charters	Canoeing—C-2 1000m
1932	Alex Wilson	400m Sprint
	Phil Edwards	800m Run
	Phil Edwards	1500m Run
	Ray Lewis, Phil Edwards, Jim Ball, Alex Wilson	4x400m Relay
	Eva Dawes	High Jump
	Noel de Mille, Charles Pratt	Rowing—Double Sculls
	Doan Boal, Earle Eastwood, Harry Fry, Joseph Harris, Cedric Liddell, George MacDonald, Stanley Stanyar, Albert Taylor, William Thoburn	Rowing—Eights
	Philip Rogers, Gerald Wilson, Gardner Boultbee, Kenneth Glass	Yachting—Team 6m
1928	Alex Wilson, Phil Edwards, Sam Glover, Jim Ball	4x400m Relay
	Ethel Smith	100m Sprint
	Jim Trifunov	Freestyle Wrestling
	Maurice Letchford	Freestyle Wrestling
	Ray Smillie	Welterweight Boxing
	Monroe Bourne, Jim Thompson, Garnet Ault, Walter Spence	4x200m Freestyle Relay Swim
	John Donnelly, Frank Fiddes, John Hand, Frederick Hedges, Athol Meech, Jack Murdock, Edgar Norris, Herbert Richardson, William Ross	Rowing—Eights
1924	Douglas Lewis	Welterweight Boxing
1920	Chris Newton	Lightweight Boxing

Summer Medal List cont.

BRONZE

Year	Athlete	Event
1920	Moe Herscovitch	Middleweight Boxing
	George Vernot	400m Freestyle Swim
1916	No Olympics due to World War I	—
1912	Frank Lukeman	Pentathlon
	Everard Butler	Rowing—Single Sculls\

Winter Olympics Medal List

GOLD

Year	Athlete	Event
2006	Chandra Crawford	Cross-country Skiing—Sprint
	Brad Gushue, Jamie Korab, Russ Howard, Mark Nichols, Mike Adam	Curling
	Jennifer Heil	Freestyle Skiing
	Canada: Meghan Agosta, Gillian Apps, Jennifer Botteril, Cassie Campbell, Gillian Ferrari, Danielle Goyette, Jayna Hefford, Becky Kellar, Gina Kingsbury, Charline Labonte, Carla Labonte, Carla MacLeod, Caroline Ouellette, Cherie Piper, Cheryl Pounder, Colleen Sostorics, Kin St-Pierre, Vicky Sunohara, Sarah Vaillancourt, Katie Weatherston, Hayley Wickenheiser	Women's Hockey
	Duff Gibson	Skeleton
	Cindy Klassen	Speed Skating—1500m
	Clara Hughes	Speed Skating—5000m

Winter Medal List cont.

GOLD

Year	Athlete	Event
2002	Canada: Ed Belfour, Rob Blake, Eric Brewer, Martin Brodeur, Theoren Fleury, Adam Foote, Simon Gagne, Jerome Iginla, Curtis Joseph, Ed Jovanovski, Paul Kariya, Mario Lemieux, Eric Lindros, Al MacInnis, Scott Niedermayer, Joe Nieuwendyk, Owen Nolan, Michael Peca, Chris Pronger, Joe Sakic, Brendan Shanahan, Ryan Smyth, Steve Yzerman	Hockey
	Canada: Dana Antal, Kelly Bechard, Jennifer Botteril, Therese Brisson, Cassie Campbell, Isabelle Chartrand, Lori Dupuis, Danielle Goyette, Geraldine Heaney, Jayna Hefford, Becky Kellar, Caroline Ouellette, Cherie Piper, Cheryl Pounder, Tammy Shewchuk, Samantha Small, Colleen Sostorics, Kim St-Pierre, Vicky Sunohara, Hayley Wickenheiser	Women's Hockey
	Jamie Sale, David Pelletier	Figure Skating—Pairs
	Catriona Le May-Doan	Speed Skating—500m
	Beckie Scott	Cross Country Skiing—10km pursuit
	Marc Gagnon	Speed Skating—Short Track 500m
	Eric Bedard, Marc Gagnon, Jonathan Guilmette, Francois-Louis Tremblay, Mathieu Turcotte	Speed Skating—Short Track 5000m Relay
1998	Dave MacEacern, Pierre Lueders	Bobsleigh—2-man
	Sandra Schmirler, Marcia Gudereit, Joan McCusker, Jan Betker, Atina Ford	Curling
	Ross Rebagliati	Snowboarding—Giant Slalom

Winter Medal List cont.

GOLD

Year	Athlete	Event
1998	Catriona Le May-Doan	Speed Skating—500m
	Annie Perreault	Speed Skating—Short track 500m
	Francois Drolet, Marc Gagnon, Jonathon Guilmette, Eric Bedard, Derrick Campbell	Speed Skating—Short Track 5000m Relay
1994	Myriam Bedard	Biathlon—7.5km
	Myriam Bedard	Biathlon—15km
	Jean-Luc Brassard	Freestyle Skiing—Moguls
1992	Angela Cutrone, Syvlie Daigle, Nathalie Lambert, Annie Perreault	Speed Skating—Short Track 3,000m Relay
	Kerrin Lee-Gartner	Alpine Skiing—Downhill
1988	No gold medals	—
1984	Gaétan Boucher	Speed Skating—1000m
	Gaétan Boucher	Speed Skating—1500m
1980	No gold medals	—
1976	Kathy Kreiner	Alpine Skiing—Giant Slalom
1972	No gold medals	—
1968	Nancy Greene	Alpine Skiing—Giant Slalom
1964	Douglas Anakin, John Emery, Vic Emery, Peter Kirby	Bobsleigh—4-man
1960	Anne Heggtveit	Alpine Skiing—Slalom

Winter Medal List cont.

GOLD

Year	Athlete	Event
1960	Barbara Wagner, Robert Paul	Figure Skating—Pairs
1956	No gold medals	
1952	Edmonton Mercurys: George Abel, Jack Davies, Billie Dawe, Bruce Dickson, Don Gauf, Bill Gibson, Ralph Hansch, Bob Meyers, Dave Miller, Eric Paterson, Tom Pollock, Al Purvis, Gordie Robertson, Louis Secco, Frank Sullivan, Bob Watt	Hockey
1948	Barbara Ann Scott	Figure Skating
	RCAF Flyers: Ross King, Andre Laperriere, Louis Lecompte, Julius Leichnitz, George Mara, Ab Renaud, Reg Schroeter, Irving Taylor, Roy Forbes, Murray Dowey, Patsy Guzzo, Orville Gravelle, Wally Halder, Andy Gilpin, Ted Hibberd, Hubert Brooks	Hockey
1944	No Olympics due to World War II	—
1940	No Olympics due to World War II	—
1936	No gold medals	—
1932	Winnipeg Hockey Club: William Cockburn, Cliff Crowley, Albert Duncanson, George Garbutt, Roy Hinkel, Vic Lundquist, Norman Malloy, Walter Monson, Ken Moore, Romeo Rivers, Harold Simpson, Hugh Sutherland, Stan Wagner, Aliston Wise	Hockey
1928	University of Toronto Grads: Charles Delahay, Frank Fisher, Grant Gordon, Louis Hudson, Norbert Mueller, Bert Plaxton, Hugh Plaxton, Roger Plaxton, John Porter, Frank Sullivan, Joseph Sullivan, Ross Taylor, Dave Trottier	Hockey
1924	Toronto Granites: Jack Cameron, Ernie Collett, Albert McCaffery, Harold McMunn, Duncan Munro, W Beattie Ramsay, Cyril Slater, Reg Smith, Harry Watson	Hockey

Winter Medal List cont.

GOLD

Year	Athlete	Event
1920	Winnipeg Falcons: Robert Benson, Wally Byron, Frank Frederikson, Chris Fridfinnson, Mike Goodman, Haldor Halderson, Konrad Johannesson, Allan Woodman*	Hockey

*The Olympic Winter Games did not officially begin until 1924 but ice hockey was included in the program for the 1920 Summer Olympic Games.

SILVER

Year	Athlete	Event
2006	Pierre Lueders, Lascelles Brown	Bobsleigh—2-man
	Beckie Scott, Sara Renner	Cross Country Skiing
	Francois-Louis Tremblay	Speed Skating—Short Track 500m
	Eric Bedard, Francois-Louis Tremblay, Charles Hamelin, Mathieu Turcotte, Jonathan Guilmette	Speed Skating—Short Track 5000m Relay
	Alanna Kraus, Anouk Leblanc-Boucher, Kalyna Roberge, Tania Vicent, Amanda Overland	Speed Skating—Short Track 3000m Relay
	Jeff Pain	Skeleton
	Arne Dankers, Steven Elm, Denny Morrison, Jason Parker, Justin Warsylewicz	Speed Skating—Team Pursuit
	Kristina Groves, Clara Hughes, Cindy Klassen, Christine Nesbitt, Shannon Rempel	Speed Skating—Team Pursuit
	Cindy Klassen	Speed Skating—1000m
	Kristina Groves	Speed Skating—1500m
2002	Kevin Martin, Don Walchuk, Carter Rycroft, Don Bartlett	Curling
	Jonathan Guillmette	Speed Skating—500m

Winter Medal List cont.

SILVER

Year	Athlete	Event
2002	Veronica Brenner	Freestyle Skiing—Aerials
1998	Jeremy Wotherspoon	Speed Skating—500m
	Susan Auch	Speed Skating—500m
	Elvis Stojko	Figure Skating—Singles
	Mike Harris, Richard Hart, Collin Mitchell, George Karrys, Paul Savage	Curling
	Canada: Jennifer Botterill, Therese Brisson, Cassie Campbell, Judy Diduck, Nancy Drolet, Lori Dupuis, Danielle Goyette, Geraldine Heaney, Jayna Hefford, Becky Kellar, Kathy McCormack, Karen Mystrom, Lesley Reddon, Manon Rheaume, Laura Schuler, Fiona Smith, France St-Louis, Vicky Sunohara, Hayley Wickenheiser, Stacy Wilson	Women's Hockey
1994	Elvis Stojko	Figure Skating—Singles
	Phillipe Laroche	Freestyle Skiing—Aerials
	Canada: Mark Astley, Adrian Aucoin, David Harlock, Corey Hirsch, Todd Hlushko, Greg Johnson, Fabian Joseph, Paul Kariya, Chris Kontos, Manny Legace, Ken Lovsin, Derek Mayer, Pter Nedved, Dwayne Norris, Greg Parks, Alain Roy, Jean-Yves Roy, Brian Savage, Brad Schlegel, Wally Schreiber, Chris Therien, Todd Warriner, Brad Werenka	Hockey
	Susan Auch	Speed Skating—500m
	Nathalie Lambert	Speed Skating—Short Track 1000m

Winter Medal List cont.

SILVER

Year	Athlete	Event
1994	Christine Boudrias, Isabelle Charest, Sylvie Daigle, Nathalie Lambert	Speed Skating— Short Track 3000m relay
1992	Canada: Dave Archibald, Todd Brost, Sean Burke, Kevin Dahl, Curt Giles, Dave Hannan, Gord Hynes, Fabian Joseph, Joe Juneau, Trevor Kidd, Patrick Lebeau, Chris Lindberg, Eric Lindros, Kent Manderville, Adrien Plavsic, Dan Ratushny, Brad Schlegel, Wally Schreiber, Randy Smith, Sam St-Laurent, Dave Tippett, Brian Tutt, Jason Wooley	Hockey
	Frederic Blackburn	Speed Skating— Short Track 1000m
	Frederic Blackburn, Michel Daignault, Mark Lackie, Sylvain Gagnon, Laurent Daigneault	Speed Skating— Short Track 5000m relay
1988	Brian Orser	Figure Skating— Singles
	Elizabeth Manley	Figure Skating— Singles
1984	Brian Orser	Figure Skating— Singles
1980	Gaétan Boucher	Speed Skating— 1000m
1976	Cathy Priestner	Speed Skating—500m
1972	Karen Magnussen	Figure Skating— Singles
1968	Nancy Greene	Alpine Skiing— Slalom
1964	No silver medals	

Winter Medal List cont.

SILVER

Year	Athlete	Event
1960	Kitchener-Waterloo Flying Dutchmen: Bobby Attersley, Maurice Benoit, James Connelly, Jack Douglas, Harold Hurley, Ken Laufmann, Floyd Martin, Robert McKnight, Cliff Pennington, Don Rope, Bobby Rousseau, George Samolenki, Harry Sinden, Darryl Sly	Hockey
1956	Frances Dafoe, Norris Bowden	Figure Skating—Pairs
1952	No silver medals	—
1948	No silver medals	—
1944	No Olympics due to World War II	—
1940	No Olympics due to World War II	—
1936	Port Arthur Bearcats: F. Maxwell Deacon, Ken Farmer, Hugh Farquharson, James Haggarty, Walter Kitchen, Ray Milton, Francis Moore, Herman Murray, Arthur Nash, Dave Neville, Ralph Saint-Germain, Alex Sinclair, William Thompson, N. Friday, G. Saxberg	Hockey
1932	Alex Hurd	Speed Skating—1500m
1928	No silver medals	—
1924	No silver medals	—

BRONZE

Year	Athlete	Event
2006	Shannon Kleibrink, Amy Nixon, Glenys Bakker, Christine Keshen, Sandra Jenkins	Curling
	Jeffrey Buttle	Figure Skating—Singles
	Anouk Leblanc-Boucher	Speed Skating—Short Track 500m
	Mellisa Richards	Skeleton

Winter Medal List cont.

BRONZE

Year	Athlete	Event
2006	Dominique Maltais	Snowboarding—Cross
	Cindy Klassen	Speed Skating—3000m
	Cindy Klassen	Speed Skating—5000m
2002	Marc Gagnon	Speed Skating—Short Track 1500m
	Kelly Law, Julie Skinner, Georgina Wheatcraft, Diane Nelson	Curling
	Deidra Dionne	Freestyle Skiing—Aerials
	Cindy Klassen	Speed Skating—3000m
	Clara Hughes	Speed Skating—5000m
2002	Mathieu Turcotte	Speed Skating—Short Track 1000m
	Alana Kraus, Marie-Eve Drolet, Amelie Goulet-Nadon, Isabelle Charest	Speed Skating—Short Track 3000m Relay
1998	Kevin Overland	Speed Skating—500m
	Eric Bedard	Speed Skating—Short track 1000m
	Christine Boudrias, Isabelle Charest, Annie Perreault, Tania Vincent	Speed Skating—Short Track 3000m Relay
	Catriona Le May-Doan	Speed Skating—1000m
1994	Edi Podivinsky	Alpine Skiing—Downhill

Winter Medal List cont.

BRONZE

Year	Athlete	Event
1994	Isabelle Brasseur, Lloyd Eisler	Figure Skating—Pairs
	Lloyd Langlois	Freestyle Skiing—Aerials
	Marc Gagnon	Speed Skating—Short Track 1000m
1992	Myriam Bedard	Biathlon—15km
	Isabelle Brasseur, Lloyd Eisler	Figure Skating—Pairs
1988	Karen Percy	Alpine Skiing—Downhill
	Karen Percy	Alpine Skiing—Super-G
	Tracy Wilson, Rob McCall	Figure Skating—Dance
1984	Gaétan Boucher	Speed Skating—500m
1980	Steve Poborski	Alpine Skiing—Downhill
1976	Toller Cranston	Figure Skating—Singles
1972	No bronze medals	
1968	Canada: Roger Bourbonnais, Ken Broderick, Ray Cadieux, Paul Conlin, Gary Dineen, Brian Glennie, Ted Hargreaves, Fran Huck, Marshall Johnston, Barry MacKenzie, Billy McMillan, Steve Monteith, Morris Mott, Terry O'Malley, Danny O'Shea, Gerry Pinder, Herb Onder, Wayne Stephenson	Hockey
1964	Debbie Wilkes, Guy Revell	Figure Skating—Pairs

Winter Medal List cont.

BRONZE

Year	Athlete	Event
1964	Petra Burka	Figure Skating—Singles
1960	Donald Jackson	Figure Skating—Singles
1956	Lucile Wheeler	Alpine Skiing—Downhill
	Kitchener—Waterloo Flying Dutchmen: Denis Brodeur, Charles Brooker, William Colvin, James Horne, Arthur Hurst, Byrle Klinck, Paul Knox, Ken Laufman, Howie Lee, James Logan, Floyd Martin, Jack MacKenzie, Don Rope, George Scholes, Gerry Theberge, Bob White, Keith Woodall	Hockey
1952	Gordon Audley	Speed Skating—500m
1948	Suzannae Morrow, Wallace Distelmeyer	Figure Skating—Pairs
1944	No Olympics due to World War II	—
1940	No Olympics due to World War II	—
1936	No bronze medals	—
1932	Montgomery Wilson	Figure Skating—Singles
	Alex Hurd	Speed Skating—500m
	William Logan	Speed Skating—1500m
	William Logan	Speed Skating—5000m
	Frank Stack	Speed Skating—10,000m
1928	No bronze medals	—
1924	No bronze medals	—

Chapter Three

Canadians in the Big Leagues

Baseball

Eric Gagne

Born in Montréal, Québec, in 1976, Eric Gagne grew up in Mascouche, just outside of the city. He learned to play both hockey and baseball with basic skills he later used as a future pitcher and Cy Young Award winner in Major League Baseball.

A former junior hockey player with scars on his hands from fights to prove it, Gagne eventually chose baseball over hockey, and in 1994 the Chicago White Sox chose him as their 30th-round draft choice. Things didn't work out with Chicago, however, and with the foresight of a Canadian scout working for the Los Angeles Dodgers, Gagne signed with the team as an amateur free agent in 1995. What's interesting at this point in Gagne's burgeoning career is that he didn't speak a word of English, only French.

Not immediately called up to play with the Dodgers after the 1995 draft, Gagne attended college in Oklahoma where he learned English and became a campus celebrity, pitching for Seminole Junior College's baseball team. Gagne played in the minor leagues of baseball until 1999, and while pitching for the San Antonio Missions of the Texas League, *Baseball Weekly* flagged Gagne as a Dodger sleeper. Finally asked to play with the team following the 1999 article, Gagne only appeared in five games as a starting pitcher. He did, however, earn the Dodger Minor League Pitcher of the Year award.

In 2000 and 2001, Gagne's time on the Dodgers pitching mound fluctuated, but with strong performances at the end of the 2001 season as a relief pitcher, 2002 was the turning point in Gagne's Major League Baseball career. He soon led the league in relief pitching, perfecting his skill with a variety of pitches, each accurate and fast. In 2003, by now thought of as a strong closer by fans of baseball, Gagne was sent out 55 times to save the game and was successful every time, becoming the first pitcher to record 50 saves in more than one season. From 2002 to 2004, "Game Over" Gagne literally saved the day 84 times in a row, a Major League Baseball record. He also became the first relief pitcher in

11 years to win the 2003 Cy Young Award. The only pitcher to win this award while in a losing season, Gagne is one of two Canadian pitchers to win baseball's highest pitching honour (the other is Ferguson Jenkins).

Gagne continued play with the Dodgers until 2005 when he underwent baseball's notorious Tommy John elbow surgery and was off for a year. He had already experienced this surgery in 1997, making him only one of a handful of pitchers to eventually return to major-league pitching after recovery. Plagued with complications from the 2005 surgery and pain in his back, Gagne was not re-signed by the Dodgers when his contract was up, and at the end of 2006, he signed with the Texas Rangers. Unfortunately, Gagne's persistent injuries resulted in his being placed on the disabled list for the third season in a row. In mid-2007, Gagne was traded to the Boston Red Sox and left at the end of the year after reaching a deal with the Milwaukee Brewers to become their new closer.

Finding it difficult to repeat his success from 2002–04, Gagne was eventually removed as the Brewers closer and finished the 2008 season with his worst full season in the major leagues. For the 2008–09 season, he re-signed with the Brewers, but in a minor-league deal.

In 2009, Gagne also had the chance to play on Team Canada in the World Baseball Classic, but it would have meant missing at least one week of training with the Brewers and a further absence if Canada advanced past the first round, which would have placed Gagne in a tricky position with Milwaukee's roster deadline. Gagne withdrew his name from Team Canada's provisional roster, stating, "I want to, but I can't. If it were a different year, maybe I would play."

Justin Morneau

Drafted to the Minnesota Twins directly out of high school, Justin Morneau, a New Westminster, BC native, is one of Major League Baseball's best first basemen. Born in 1981, Morneau played basketball, baseball and hockey throughout high school and in 1998 played on the Memorial Cup–winning junior-AAA Portland Winterhawks team as a goalie. He was also a member of the Canadian National Champion baseball team in 1997 and 1998—the latter in which he was named the best hitter and catcher of the competition.

Graduating high school in 1999, Morneau decided to stick with baseball as his primary sport and was soon selected in the third round as the 89th-overall pick by the Minnesota Twins in the Major League Baseball Amateur Entry Draft of that same year. Playing in the minor leagues for four years, Morneau made his debut with the Twins in June 2003. He was sent back down to the minor leagues shortly afterward, but put together impressive statistics, and when the Twins dealt a first baseman to the Boston Red Sox in 2004, Morneau stepped up as starter. Unfortunately, the following 2005 season proved to be challenging for Morneau: in the winter he suffered from appendicitis, the chicken pox, pleurisy and pneumonia, and he also got hit in the head by a pitch in April.

Prior to the 2006 season, a recovered Morneau played for Canada in that year's World Baseball Classic and soon came into his own with the Twins. Consistently near the top of the American League leaderboard in batting average, home runs and RBI, in August 2006 Morneau became the first Minnesota player since 1987 to hit 30 home runs in one season. He finished 2006 second in the league in RBI, tied with Larry Walker's 1997 total for the most RBI in a season by a Canadian. He also won the American League Silver Slugger Award and American League MVP Award, beating out Derek Jeter of the New York Yankees for the latter. Morneau was officially the first Canadian to win the American League MVP Award, the second to win a major-league

MVP award and the fourth Minnesota Twin to take home the honour.

Continuing his spectacular play through 2007, at the beginning of the 2008 season, Morneau signed a six-year contract with the Minnesota Twins worth $80 million, the longest and richest contract in the franchise's history. Proving his worth, Morneau won the 2008 Home Run Derby—the first Canadian to ever win the event. His feat did not go unrecognized in Canada, and he was awarded with the Lionel Conacher Award in 2008, beating out Sidney Crosby. Only the third baseball player to win the award, Morneau said, "Any time you can beat out a hockey player in anything in Canada, it's an accomplishment."

Hockey remains near and dear to Morneau's heart, however, and he wears the number 33 in honour of his idol, former NHL goalie Patrick Roy, and up until the end of the 2008 baseball season wore a Todd Bertuzzi Vancouver Canucks T-shirt under his jersey during every game since the shirt was given to him in 2006. Part of Morneau's repertoire of superstitions that includes eating macaroni and cheese before every game, he kept the Bertuzzi T-shirt around because the Twins started winning and Morneau began to hit around the time he started wearing it.

"There's some superstition involved," Morneau has said, but whether it's divine intervention or pure skill, Morneau has proved he belongs in the big leagues.

Record-breaking Fact

The first Canadian to play Major League Baseball was Bill Phillips from Saint John, New Brunswick. Between 1879 and 1888, Phillips was a member of the Cleveland Blues, the Brooklyn Grays and the Kansas City Cowboys.

Jason Bay

Emerging as Canada's first Rookie of the Year in Major League Baseball, Jason Bay has spent his life devoted to the sport. Born in Trail, BC, his path to big-league success began with his 22nd-round draft to the Montréal Expos in 2000. However, he never played a major-league game with the Expos and was dealt to the New York Mets in 2002. Before the end of that year's trade deadline, Bay was moved yet again, traded to the San Diego Padres. He made his major-league debut in 2003, but two days later his right wrist was broken when he got in the way of a pitch. Bay moved cities yet again, traded to the Pittsburgh Pirates mid-season in 2003.

It turned out that 2004 with the Pirates was to be Bay's breakout year, and he went on to produce the best offensive numbers of any National League rookie that year. Bay led the rookies in home runs, RBI, slugging percentage, extra base hits and total bases. He also broke the Pirates' rookie record from 1946 for home runs with a total of 26. Honoured with the 2004 National League Rookie of the Year Award, Bay was the first Canadian to ever achieve this win.

Bay continued to lead the Pirates in every major hitting category in 2005 and also set a new record for most games played in a major-league season by a Canadian. And, in 2006, he became the first member of the Pirates to be voted into the All-Star game as a starter since Andy Van Slyke in 1993. Bay stayed with the Pirates through to the end of the 2008 season when he was traded with Josh Wilson in a highly publicized three-team deal with the Boston Red Sox and Los Angeles Dodgers that saw Bay and Wilson go to the Red Sox, Red Sox player Manny Ramirez to the Dodgers, Dodgers Andy LaRoche and Bryan Morris to the Pirates and Red Sox players Brandon Moss and Craig Hansen to the Pirates.

Bay's new position with the Red Sox sent his hometown of Trail into a frenzy. Bay later remarked, "No one was happier than him [my father] when I got traded over here. All these people where I'm from, Trail, 8000 people, went, 'Oh, I love the Red Sox.'" Bay will find further support from Canada in 2009 when he plays on Team Canada in the World Baseball Classic in the opening game against the U.S. at the Rogers Centre in Toronto. Showing how Bay's pride in Canada has never waned, he says of the tournament:

> *It's a little bit different when you've got Canada on your chest [rather than] Boston Red Sox or whatever team. There's just that little extra national pride that goes into it—something you can't simulate.*

Larry Walker

Canada's first National League MVP and MVP winner in either major baseball league, Larry Walker, a Maple Ridge, BC native, has a firm place in Canada's baseball history. Signed with the Montréal Expos as an amateur free agent in 1984, this right fielder played in the minor leagues until his major-league debut in 1989. It didn't take long for Walker to establish himself as an above-average hitter, and Walker, along with the Expos of 1994, were thought to be World Series contenders until the players' strike of that year. It was Walker's last season with the Expos, and he signed with the Colorado Rockies in 1995. In his first year with the Rockies, Walker's batting skills were enough to place him in the top 10 in numerous offensive categories for the Rockies, and it was with Colorado that he became the first Canadian player to win the National League MVP Award, thanks to a phenomenal season in 1997 with a 0.366 batting average, 49 home runs, 130 RBI, 33 stolen bases, 409 total bases and 12 outfield assists. With the MVP win, Walker was also the first player of a non-playoff team (excluding the 1994 strike season) to take the award since Major League Baseball became two three-division leagues. In recognizing his accomplishments, Walker was awarded the 1998 Lou Marsh Trophy as Canada's Athlete of the Year after being runner-up to race-car driver Jacques Villeneuve the year earlier.

In the following years, Walker continued to play well, surpassing Jeff Heath in 2000 as the Canadian all-time hits leader, but he also suffered from repeated injuries and never again matched his 1997 season. Nine years after signing with the Rockies, Walker jumped to the St. Louis Cardinals in 2004 in a trade for three minor-league players. One year later, defeated in the National League Championship series by the Houston Astros, Walker's career was over. He retired before the 2006 season, walking away with the most home runs ever hit by a Canadian in the major leagues, seven Gold

Glove Awards, three Silver Slugger Awards and a never-before-seen nine Tip O'Neill Awards as Canadian baseball player of the year. Walker was inducted into Canada's Sports Hall of Fame in 2007 and as of 2009 spends his time with his family and works part time for the Cardinals.

Lou Marsh Trophy

Awarded annually to Canada's top athlete, professional or amateur, the Lou Marsh Trophy winner is decided upon by a panel of journalists. The trophy is named after the late Lou Marsh, who was a well-known Canadian athlete and referee as well as sports editor of the *Toronto Star*.

Lou Marsh Trophy Winners

Year	Winner	Sport	Number of Wins
2008	Chantal Petitclerc	Wheelchair Racing	1
2007	Sidney Crosby	Hockey	1
2006	Cindy Klassen	Speed Skating	1
2005	Steve Nash	Basketball	1
2004	Adam van Koeverden	Kayaking	1
2003	Mike Weir	Golf	1
2002	Catriona Le May-Doan	Speed Skating	1
2001	Jamie Salé & David Pelletier	Figure Skating	1
2000	Daniel Igali	Wrestling	1
1999	Caroline Brunet	Kayaking	1

Lou Marsh Winners cont.

Year	Winner	Sport	Number of Wins
1998	Larry Walker	Baseball	1
1997	Jacques Villeneuve	Auto Racing	2
1996	Donovan Bailey	Track and Field	1
1995	Jacques Villeneuve	Auto Racing	1
1994	Myriam Bédard	Biathlon	1
1993	Mario Lemieux	Hockey	1
1992	Mark Tewksbury	Swimming	1
1991	Silken Laumann	Rowing	1
1990	Kurt Browning	Figure Skating	1
1989	Wayne Gretzky	Hockey	4
1988	Carolyn Waldo	Synchronized Swimming	1
1987	Ben Johnson	Track and Field	2
1986	Ben Johnson	Track and Field	1
1985	Wayne Gretzky	Hockey	3
1984	Gaétan Boucher	Speed Skating	1
1983	Wayne Gretzky	Hockey	2
1983	Rick Hansen	Wheelchair Racing	1
1982	Wayne Gretzky	Hockey	1
1981	Susan Nattrass	Shooting	1
1980	Terry Fox	Marathon of Hope	1
1979	Sandra Post	Golf	1
1978	Ken Read	Alpine Skiing	1
1978	Graham Smith	Swimming	1
1977	Guy Lafleur	Hockey	1
1976	Sandy Hawley	Horse Racing	2
1975	Bobby Clarke	Hockey	1
1974	Ferguson Jenkins	Baseball	1
1973	Sandy Hawley	Horse Racing	1
1972	Phil Esposito	Hockey	1

Canadian Sports Records

Lou Marsh Winners cont.

Year	Winner	Sport	Number of Wins
1971	Hervé Filion	Harness Racing	1
1970	Bobby Orr	Hockey	1
1969	Russ Jackson	Football	1
1968	Nancy Greene	Alpine Skiing	2
1967	Nancy Greene	Alpine Skiing	1
1966	Elaine Tanner	Swimming	1
1965	Petra Burka	Figure Skating	1
1964	Roger Jackson and George Hungerford	Rowing	1
1963	Bill Crothers	Track and Field	1
1962	Donald Jackson	Figure Skating	1
1961	Bruce Kidd	Track and Field	1
1960	Anne Heggtveit	Alpine Skiing	1
1959	Barbara Wagner & Bob Paul	Figure Skating	1
1958	Lucile Wheeler	Alpine Skiing	1
1957	Maurice Richard	Hockey	1
1956	Marlene Streit	Golf	2
1955	Beth Whittall	Swimming	1
1954	Marilyn Bell	Swimming	1
1953	Doug Hepburn	Weightlifting	1
1952	George Genereux	Shooting	1
1951	Marlene Streit	Golf	1
1950	Bob McFarlane	Football and Track and Field	1
1949	Cliff Lumsdon	Swimming	1
1948	Barbara Ann Scott	Figure Skating	3
1947	Barbara Ann Scott	Figure Skating	2
1946	Joe Krol	Football	1
1945	Barbara Ann Scott	Figure Skating	1

Lou Marsh Winners cont.			
Year	Winner	Sport	Number of Wins
1944	No winner because of World War II		—
1943	No winner because of World War II		—
1942	No winner because of World War II		—
1941	Theo Dubois	Rowing	1
1940	Gérard Côté	Marathon	1
1939	Bob Pirie	Swimming	1
1938	Henry "Bobby" Pearce	Rowing	1
1937	Marshall Cleland	Equestrian	1
1936	Phil Edwards	Track and Field	1

Football

With some of Canadian sport's most rabid fans, the Canadian Football League's eight teams create heated debate across the country every regular season, playoff season, pre-season and post-season. Next to only the NHL in sport popularity among Canadians, the end of each CFL season culminates in the taking of the Grey Cup, North America's second-oldest sports trophy.

Canadian pride in the CFL is rampant, as is showcased in the Canadian Football Hall of Fame in Hamilton, Ontario, and many players find their lifelong niche in the league. As described by football great Mike Pringle later in this chapter, he wouldn't trade his time in the CFL for anything else, joining the ranks of many who found their glory in Canadian football.

The record-breakers in this section include both Canadians and Americans, but nationality has not mattered to Canadians who have taken these players in as their own.

Doug Flutie

Eventually making his way to Canada to leave his mark in the history of the CFL, Doug Flutie was born in Maryland in the U.S. He got his start in football in high school, progressing on to Boston College, where he left behind a record as the NCAA's all-time passing-yardage leader. The 1984 Heisman Trophy award-winner in his final year of college, Flutie went on to play with the New Jersey Generals in the now-defunct United States Football League, was drafted to the NFL Los Angeles Rams—where he stayed on the practice roster—and then played with the Chicago Bears and New England Patriots. Coming to Canada in 1990, signed with the BC Lions, Flutie began his illustrious career north of the U.S. border with, at the time, the highest salary in the league. Traded to the Calgary Stampeders only one year after signing with the Lions, Flutie, a star quarterback, led his team to a Grey Cup victory in 1992—a win he counts as his biggest sports thrill. Flutie was a Stampeder until 1996 but didn't leave without first throwing a record 48 touchdown passes.

His next stop on the CFL circuit was in Toronto with the Argonauts. Leading Toronto to consecutive Grey Cup wins in 1996 and 1997, Flutie received his third and final Grey Cup MVP in the 1997 playoffs.

Flutie returned to the NFL in 1998 and left behind a CFL record for most outstanding player wins, with six between 1991 and 1997. The only year he missed was 1995. He also holds the record of 6619 yards passing in a single season, four of the CFL's top-five highest single-season completion marks, including a record 466 in 1991, and the record for touchdown passes in a season (1994), with 48. Flutie owns league and franchise records with each CFL team he has played for.

Groomed well in his years in Canada, Flutie joined the Buffalo Bills five games into the 1998 NFL season. His talent was quickly recognized, and he became Pro Bowl and NFL Comeback Player of the Year. In 2005 at the age of 43, Flutie was also a member of the San Diego Chargers and the New England Patriots, with whom he ended his football career.

Despite leaving Canada in the late 1990s, Flutie's prowess on the gridiron was never forgotten, and as recently as 2006 he was named number one in a TSN list of the top-50 CFL players. Of this honour, Flutie said:

I'm flattered and humbled to be selected…
I thoroughly enjoyed my time in the CFL and have
nothing but the highest respect for those who pre-
ceded me in the history of the league and those
who have followed.

One year later, Flutie was inducted into Canada's Sports Hall of Fame, the first non-Canadian to be inducted. And in 2008—his first year of eligibility—Flutie was elected to the Canadian Football Hall of Fame.

Mike Pringle

Also born in the U.S., this California export made a name for himself in Canada during his 15-year career in the CFL. Mike Pringle tied or broke almost every rushing record in the league and is known as one of the greatest players in his position to ever play in the CFL.

Pringle started out in football in high school and went on to join the team at California State University, Fullerton. His skill was apparent and he was chosen 139th overall by the Atlanta Falcons in the 1990 NFL Draft. Pringle never played a game with the Falcons and was kept on the practice roster for the entire season. Cut from the team, Pringle entered the CFL in 1992 with the Edmonton Eskimos. The team kept him for only three games before releasing him, and Pringle spent the rest of 1992 with the Sacramento Surge in the World League of American Football (WLAF). He left the WLAF in 1993 to end up with a Canadian team—the Sacramento Gold Miners, the first American team in the CFL. Pringle's second stint in Sacramento only lasted one season until he was traded to the Baltimore Stallions, also a CFL team at that time.

The Stallions obtained Pringle for the 1994 season, and it was with Baltimore that this beleaguered running back was finally able to prove his talent. He ran a then-record 1972 yards with 13 touchdowns, coming up just shy of earning the right to call himself the first CFL running back to obtain 2000 yards rushing. In the 1994 season, fans also saw Pringle lead the Stallions to their first Grey Cup championship game. They lost to the BC Lions but were back again in 1995 against the Calgary Stampeders, where Pringle and his team took the Cup.

The NFL came calling again in 1996, and Pringle signed with the Denver Broncos, only to get cut in training camp and return to the Stallions roster for the remainder of the '96 season. Pringle followed his Baltimore team to its new location in Montréal, as the Alouettes, and saw glory there in 1997 and 1998. With crowds coming out just to see Pringle play, in 1998 he had 2065 rushing yards—a CFL record. As of 2009, he remains the only player in the league to ever run for 2000 yards. Pringle stayed with the Alouettes until the end of the 2002 season, throughout which time he continued to put up impressive numbers. He was also part of Montréal's Grey Cup win in 2002 but argued with head coach Don Matthews about not being used as starter in the game and soon left for Edmonton.

Thought to be past his peak by many in the sports world, by the time the 2003 season was finished, Pringle proved he was no slouch, helping the Eskimos to a Grey Cup win that year. And in 2004, Pringle broke the CFL record for career rushing yards with 16,425. In the last game of the season, he was also within an inch of breaking the CFL record for career rushing touchdowns—in fact, he was tied for the record and only needed one more rushing touchdown to surpass George Reed. Pringle, however, found himself embroiled in another argument with his head coach when Tom Higgins called a pass play that resulted in a score. As a result, Higgins' decision caused Pringle to end the 2004 season tied with the standing career-rushing-touchdowns record he wanted to break

Leaving Edmonton, Pringle unofficially retired at the end of the 2004 season, but signed a contract with Montréal in 2005. He then officially retired so he could do so as a member of the Alouettes. One day later, Pringle's jersey number (27) was also retired at the team's first game of the season.

Pringle finished fourth in TSN's 2006 list of the Top 50 CFL players, and in 2008 was inducted into the Canadian Football Hall of Fame in his first year of eligibility. He also remains the record holder for most rushing yards (all-time, regular season), most 100+ rushing games (regular season), most consecutive 100+ yards rushing games (regular season) and most rushing attempts (regular season). Interviewed by the *Los Angeles Times* in 2008, Pringle didn't have any regrets about spending the bulk of his pro football career in Canada:

> *The fact that I was able to play football for a living for 15 years, I wouldn't change anything. If they said, "You can have six years in the NFL instead of your entire career in the CFL," I wouldn't take it. I love what I was able to accomplish, the people I met, the experiences… I enjoyed myself. I really had a good time.*

Damon Allen

Yet another American expatriate making a name for himself in Canada's football league,

California-born quarterback Damon Allen leads the all-time pro football (CFL and NFL) passing chart with 72,381 passing yards, a record he reached while playing for the Toronto Argonauts.

The younger brother of NFL star Marcus Allen, Damon always had football in his blood and started playing at the age of six. He spent his amateur career with California State University, Fullerton, where he broke seven of the school's records. Balancing another career in baseball, Allen was drafted to the Detroit Tigers in 1984, never signing a major-league contract with the team, but keeping both baseball and football in his life for nine more years.

Allen joined the Edmonton Eskimos as a free agent in 1985 and was a hit right off the bat. Displaying impressive rookie and sophomore seasons, Allen stepped in for injured starter Matt Dunnigan in the 1987 Grey Cup game, leading the Eskimos to victory. He spent one more year with Edmonton, signing with the Ottawa Rough Riders in 1989. Three years later, Allen moved to the Hamilton Tiger-Cats, only to be traded back to the Eskimos in 1993. It was also in this year that Allen pushed aside his possible Major League Baseball career after signing with the Pittsburgh Pirates and reporting for training camp, but then deciding to stick with football.

And so, back in Edmonton again, it was as if he had never left and for a second time helped lead the team to a Grey Cup victory. Two years later Allen signed with the CFL pet project the Memphis Mad Dogs, a team that was part of the attempted CFL expansion into the U.S. The Mad Dogs remained a team for only one season, so Allen moved on yet again, this time to join the BC Lions in 1996.

By this point is his career, Allen had won two Grey Cup Most Valuable Player awards and had shown a definite presence on the field. Voted to the CFL's West Division All-Star team in 1999, he went on to become the league's all-time leading passer in 2000, as well as the Lions' Most Outstanding Player that year. A year later, Allen became the first CFL quarterback to rush for over 10,000 yards. Traded from the Lions in 2003, Allen settled in with the Toronto Argonauts, where he spent the rest of his career.

Surpassing the record for most career touchdown passes in the CFL and approaching age 40, Allen showed no signs of slowing down until he fractured his left tibia in a game against Montréal in 2004. He came back to CFL action only eight weeks after the injury and soon became the second quarterback in Argonaut history to complete more than 12 consecutive passes in a game. He also experienced both his third Grey Cup win and Grey Cup Most Valuable Player award.

In 2005, Allen received his first CFL Outstanding Player Award, but at the start of the 2006 season was on the bench for a short time because of a broken finger on his right hand. Never one to idle for long, Allen was soon back on the field for the rest of the season and broke the record to become pro football's all-time passing leader. During the game in which Allen broke the record, then-CFL commissioner Tom Wright halted play for a presentation in Allen's honour.

After reaching this peak in 2006, Allen's career started to decline, with his previously broken finger and an injury to his toe causing further strife in 2007. He officially retired from football in 2008, but remained employed with the Argos as a special adviser to CEO Michael "Pinball" Clemons. Upon retiring, Allen said:

The game of football has given me every emotion a person can feel. It has been a dream ride...
I want to thank the fans across the Canadian Football League for supporting me, the players in the CFL for challenging me to be the best and the incredible coaches in our league that continue to teach the game.

Lui Passaglia

Born in 1954 in Vancouver, BC, Lui Passaglia has proved to be one of the brightest stars in the history of the CFL. Starting his amateur football career at Simon Fraser University in BC, he played the position of wide receiver as well as kicker/punter when the situation demanded it. And it was in the kicker role where Passaglia excelled, creating the foundation for his long career in Canadian football. The fifth pick overall by the BC Lions in 1976, Passaglia never left the team, spending his entire 25-year pro career with the Lions. Setting a record for longevity as the only player to have played that many seasons with the CFL, Passaglia's record breaking doesn't end there. Nine-time winner of the CFL Western Division All-Star award, four-time winner of the CFL All-Star award and one-time winner of the Grey Cup Most Valuable Canadian Award, Passaglia's total accomplishments in the CFL are unparalleled by any other player.

He holds the regular-season CFL records for most regular-season games (408), scored points in regular-season play (3991), most converts (1014), most field goals (875), best field-goal percentage in a season (90.9 percent) and most single points (309). Passaglia is also the all-time punt leader with 3142 punts for 133,826 yards, with the highest average in a season of 50.2 yards in 1983. In the playoff-season record books, he holds for the records for most points (210) and longest punt (89 yards). Additionally, he was the first CFL player to score 200 points in a season, with 214 in 1987.

Passaglia's career came to the perfect end in 2000 in the Grey Cup game against the Calgary Stampeders. He kicked his last point in the CFL—a 29-yard field goal that turned out to be the game winner. Since retiring, Passaglia has been inducted into the BC Sports Hall of Fame, the Canadian Football Hall of Fame and had his number 5 jersey retired by the Lions. Never one to stray far from home, Passaglia has remained in BC and works as the director of community relations for the BC Lions.

George Reed

Inducted into the Canadian Football Hall of Fame in 1979, and before the likes of Doug Flutie came along, George Reed made his presence known in the CFL. Voted one point behind Flutie as number two in TSN's 2006 list of the CFL's top-50 players, this U.S.-born running back became famous in Canadian sport.

Signing with the Saskatchewan Roughriders straight from Washington State University in

1963, Reed remained with the Roughriders for the duration of his 13-year CFL career. Upon arriving in Regina for his first CFL training camp, Reed said:

Regina wasn't really clearly marked. Where the overpass was on Albert Street now, it used to be a four-way stop. I came to the four-way stop. I guess I had missed the sign saying "Regina" and if there was a sign, it was a very small sign.

Reed played 203 games with the Roughriders, and by 1975—his last year in pro football—had career records in 1000-yard rushing seasons, rushing yards, rushing touchdowns and touchdowns. His 1000-yard rushing seasons and rushing touchdowns records still stand in the CFL as recently as 2009.

While still a player in the league, as well as after his retirement, Reed was president of the CFL Players' Association, and a year after retiring, was awarded the first Tom Pate Memorial Trophy for playing ability and community service. Ultimately, Reed walked away from pro football as a leader in CFL history, capturing over 15 regular-season records and over five playoff records. At his retirement ceremony, he was humble and was quoted as saying:

I don't know what to say—really. You are honouring an athlete who really deserves no honour.

*I came to play football, got paid to play and then
I tried to merge into the community.*

Reed was honoured with an Order of Canada in 1978, an award made even more notable because he was an American. He chose to make Canada his permanent home, however, and in 2009 accepted a position as corporate event host for Casino Regina and Casino Moose Jaw. Moving back to Saskatchewan from Alberta, Reed said he was "thrilled" to be coming back to the province where he has "so many fond memories."

CFL Records

Record		Athlete	Year
Most touchdowns in a game	6	Bob McNamara	1956
	6	Eddie James	1932
Most touchdowns in a season	23	Milt Stegall	2002
Most passing touchdowns in a game	8	Joe Zuger	1962
Most passing touchdowns in a season	48	Doug Flutie	1994
Most career passing touchdowns	394	Damon Allen	—
Most career touchdowns	144	Milt Stegall	—
Most rushing touchdowns in a game	5	Earl Lunsford	1962
	5	Martin Patton	1995
Most rushing touchdowns in a season	19	Mike Pringle	2000
Most career rushing touchdowns	134	George Reed	—
Most receiving touchdowns in a game	5	Ernie Pitts	1959
Most receiving touchdowns in a season	23	Milt Stegall	2002
Most career receiving touchdowns	141	Milt Stegall	—
Most punt return touchdowns in a season	5	Henry Williams	1991

CFL Records cont.

Record		Athlete	Year
Most career punt return touchdowns	26	Henry Williams	1991
Most career kick return touchdowns	5	Harvey Wylie	—
Most interception return touchdowns in a game	3	Vernon Mitchell	2000
Most interception return touchdowns in a season	5	Malcolm Frank	2004
Most career interception return touchdowns	8	Dick Thornton	—
	8	Malcolm Frank	—
Most rushing yards in a game	287	Ron Stewart	1960
Most rushing yards in a season	2065	Mike Pringle	1998
Most career rushing yards	16,425	Mike Pringle	—
Longest rush in a game	109	George Dixon	1963
	109	Willie Fleming	1964
Most rushing attempts in a game	37	Doyle Orange	1975
Most rushing attempts in a season	347	Mike Pringle	1998
Most career rushing attempts	3243	George Reed	—
Most passing yards in a game	713	Matt Dunigan	1994
Most passing yards in a season	6619	Doug Flutie	1991
Most career passing yards	72,381	Damon Allen	—
Highest pass completion in a game	90.9	Casey Printers	2004
Highest pass completion in a season	73.98	Dave Dickenson	2005
High career pass completion	67.6	Dave Dickenson	—
Most receiving yards in a game	338	Hal Patterson	1956
Most receiving yards in a season	2036	Allen Pitts	1994
Most career receiving yards	14,891	Allen Pitts	—
Most pass receptions in a season	160	Derrel Mitchell	1998
Most career pass receptions	1006	Terry Vaughn	—
Most interceptions in a season	15	Al Brenner	1972
Most career interceptions	87	Less Browne	—

CFL Records cont.

Record		Athlete	Year
Most interception return yards in a game	172	Barry Ardern	1969
Most interception return yards in a season	348	Byron Parker	2006
Most career interception return yards	1508	Less Browne	—
Longest interception return	120	Neal Beaumont	1963
Most kickoff return yards in a game	257	Anthony Cherry	1989
Most kickoff return yards in a season	1695	Eric Blount	1998
Most career kickoff return yards	7354	Henry Williams	—
Most kickoff returns in a season	64	Eric Blount	1998
Most career kickoff returns	335	Henry Williams	—
Most punt return yards in a game	232	Henry Williams	1991
Most punt return yards in a season	1440	Henry Williams	1991
Most career punt return yards	11,177	Henry Williams	—
Most punt returns in a season	123	Jim Silye	1970
Most career punt returns	1003	Henry Williams	—
Longest punt return	131	Boyd Carter, Dave Mann	1958
Most punts in a game	18	Martin Fabi	1963
Most punts in a season	188	Bob Cameron	1988
Most career punts	3142	Lui Passaglia	—
Most punt yards in a game	814	Martin Fabi	1963
Most punt yards in a season	8214	Bob Cameron	1988
Most career punt yards	134,301	Bob Cameron	—
Highest punting average in a game	63.5	Paul Osbaldiston	2002
Highest punting average in a season	50.6	Jon Ryan	2005
Highest career punting average	46.4	Noel Prefontaine	—
Longest punt	108	Zenon Andrusyshyn	1977
Most field goals in a season	59	Dave Ridgeway	1990
Most career field goals	875	Lui Passaglia	—

CFL Records cont.			
Record		**Athlete**	**Year**
Longest field goal	62	Paul McCallum	2001
Highest career field goal accuracy	82.35	Sandro DeAngelis	—
Most tackles in a game	16	Reggie Hunt	2003
Most tackles in a season	129	Calvin Tiggle	1994
Most career tackles	1241	Willie Pless	—
Most fumble return yards in a season	182	Reggie Givens	1997
Most career fumble return yards	270	Greg Battle	—
Longest fumble return	104	Al Washington	1984
Most sacks in a season	26.5	James Parker	1984
Most career sacks	157	Grover Covington	—
Most blocked kicks in a season	5	James Zachary	1986
Most career blocked kicks	12	Gerald Vaughn	—

Motorsports

Gilles Villeneuve

Gilles Villeneuve is, simply, one of Canada's—and the world's—most revered race-car drivers. Born in Richelieu, Québec, in 1950 and growing up in Berthierville, Québec, he always felt the need for speed, beginning his race-car career in local drag-racing events in his self-modified Ford Mustang. But this type of racing was not enough for Villeneuve, and he obtained a racing licence from the Jim Russell Racing School at Le Circuit Mont Tremblant. He won 7 of the 10 Formula Ford races he entered with them, and Villeneuve soon began to participate in Formula Atlantic racing. Between 1975 and 1977, he won his first race—in heavy rain—dominated the 1976 season by winning all but one race, took the U.S. and Canadian titles that same year and won the Canadian championship again in 1977. Throughout this time, Villeneuve supported his debts by snowmobile racing, taking the world title in the 440-cc division.

However, Villeneuve's style on the track eventually caught the attention of several Grand Prix stars, and in 1976 the McLaren racing team offered Villeneuve a Formula 1 deal; he made his debut at the 1977 British Grand Prix.

Despite his promise, or perhaps because of it, McLaren's team manager decided to release Villeneuve because he "was looking as though he might be a bit expensive." Luckily for Villeneuve, the power of word of mouth found him sitting in front of Ferrari team founder Enzo Ferrari in no time. After completing a session that saw Villeneuve make mistakes and set slow times at Ferrari's Fiorano test track, Enzo chose to sign Villeneuve, regardless, for the end of the 1977 season and the entire 1978 season. It was with Ferrari that Villeneuve captured his first Grand Prix win—at the Canadian Grand Prix in 1978. As of 2009, he is the last Canadian to top the homeland race, and Villeneuve later called the win "the happiest day of my life." The result of the Canadian Grand Prix was "Villeneuve Fever" in Canada, and he went on to win the Grand Prix of Monaco and Spain, with some calling him the best driver on the circuit. He was also the champion of the Jarama Grand Prix, and following the win, *Time* magazine dedicated its August 31, 1981, edition to him; the only other driver to ever receive this honour was Jim Clark.

In 1982, however, everything came to a tragic halt. While at the Belgian Grand Prix, Villeneuve headed back out onto the track to better his original qualifying time; it is thought he wanted to beat the time of current rival teammate Didier Pironi. On his second lap, Villeneuve ran into a slower-moving car belonging to Jochen Mass, and Villeneuve's car was launched into the air at a speed estimated between 200 and 225 kilometres per hour. The car flew 100 metres and disintegrated upon contact with the ground. Villeneuve was thrown a further 50 metres from the wreck into a fence. Drivers and doctors rushed to the scene and Villeneuve was sent to hospital with a fractured neck, an injury that took his life that same evening.

Then prime minister Pierre Trudeau and Opposition leader Joe Clark led the mourners at Villeneuve's funeral, and his service was broadcast live, coast-to-coast. Villeneuve's all-or-nothing style has never been forgotten and he has a host of honours. Since his death, the Gilles Villeneuve Museum has been erected in his hometown of Berthierville; the Autodromo Enzo e Dino Ferrari racing venue in Italy named a corner after him; a Canadian flag was painted on the third slot of the starting grid where he began his last race and the corner of the track where he died was turned into a chicane and named after him; a bronze bust was made of him at the entrance to the Ferrari test track at Fiorano; the racetrack in Montréal used for the Canadian Grand Prix was named in his honour; he has been inducted into the Canadian Motorsport Hall of Fame; Canada Post released a postage stamp with his likeness; and he has been put on the cover of Britain's respected *MotorSport* magazine. Perhaps his best accomplishment, however, was his son, Jacques Villeneuve, who followed his father into the world of motorsports, with great success.

Jacques Villeneuve

As if the legend of his father wasn't enough, Jacques Villeneuve was bitten by the racing bug when, at 14 years old, his mother allowed him to drive a 100-cc kart around the kart track at Imola in Italy. That same day he progressed into a 135-cc kart and ended with a Formula 4 car on the Grand Prix track. The Québec-born Villeneuve, who was raised in Monaco, was soon enrolled by his uncle, other famed racer Jacques Villeneuve Sr., in the same driving school Gilles once attended: the Jim Russell Driving School. Jacque's instructor called him the best student he had ever seen. Spending the following summer of 1987 under the tuition of former Jim Russell Driving School instructor Richard Spenard, Villeneuve learned to hone his craft and was soon making his racing debut in 1988 driving a touring car at the Italian Championship. He stayed in Italy until 1992 when he moved to Japan to compete with Toyota's prestigious Formula 3 team. That year also saw Villeneuve come back to Canada to race in a one-off Formula Atlantic event in Trois-Rivières, Québec. From there, his career truly took off, with his agent quickly steering him from Formula Atlantic to IndyCar to Formula 1 racing.

Competing in the Indianapolis 500 in 1994, Villeneuve held the record—at the time—for the fastest lap ever by a rookie, and in light of this and other successes that year, Villeneuve ended up as IndyCar racing's 1994 Rookie of the Year. On his second attempt at Indianapolis in 1995, he took the crown—at 24 years old, Villeneuve was officially the youngest-ever IndyCar champion and youngest driver to win the Indianapolis 500.

The following year, Villeneuve came close to becoming only the third person to win a rookie Grand Prix at the 1996 Melbourne event. He did, however, equal three other racers as the only drivers to achieve pole position in their first race. His accomplishments didn't stop there—he was also the winner of the 1997 Formula 1 World Championship, introducing him to a group of just four other racers who had won both the Formula 1 and IndyCar titles. No other Canadian has won these two titles. Villeneuve's father was never far from his mind during this time: "My father was a legend," said Villeneuve. "He'll always be the first Canadian to win a Grand Prix, to make it to the top, and he'll always stay there."

Riding high on his success, Villeneuve appeared in 1997 in a commercial with Canadian Olympic sprinter Donovan Bailey that proclaimed Canada "the fastest nation on earth." This was the last year in which Villeneuve saw the podium; although continuing to race, he has never again achieved the success he did in the 1990s.

Most notably in the new millennium, Villeneuve was one of Peugeot Sport's nine drivers in the 2007 and 2008 24 Hours of Le Mans events. In 2008, Villeneuve and his team finished second, with Villeneuve pledging to keep competing in the event until he wins it. If he were to win the competition, he would become only the second person to win the triple crown of motorsports: the Indianapolis 500, Formula 1 World Championship and 24 Hours of Le Mans.

Whether he wins or not, Villeneuve is still a hero in Canada and was among the first group inducted onto Canada's Walk of Fame. He was also awarded the Lou Marsh Trophy for Athlete of the Year in both 1995 and 1997.

Paul Tracy

No stranger to the spotlight, this West Hill, Ontario native found fame at an early age in 1986, becoming the youngest Canadian Formula Ford champion in history at 16 years old. At age 18, he also won the Can-Am race, the youngest winner in the race's history. "The Thrill From West Hill," he immediately went on to hold the then-series records at the PPG-Dayton Indy Lights championship for victories (nine) and poles (seven) in 14 events. Such success saw him receive the Bruce McLaren Trophy, presented by the British Racing Drivers' Club, as the Commonwealth's most promising driver in 1990.

Making his way through the ranks of racing on the IndyCar Penske team, he moved to Newman/Haas Racing in 1995 only to return to Penske in 1996. It was this year Tracy set a track record at Nazareth to become the first driver in ChampCar history to break 305 kilometres per hour on a one-mile oval. Not a man to stay in one place for long, Tracy left Penske again to race for Team KOOL Green in the 1998 season and ended up having one of the best years of his career with them in 1999. Tracy was named part of the inaugural five-member CART All-Star team, achieved a career-best in points and starts, and reached the podium seven times. He also had an impressive year in 2000 with Team Green, setting the track record at pole position at the Michigan 500 with a speed of 378 kilometres per hour. He also recorded a victory at Long Beach, beginning at the 17th starting position, which represented the second-deepest spot on the starting grid from which anyone had driven to a win on a road or street course in CART history.

Leaving Team Green for Player's/Forsythe in 2003, Tracy drove to one of the top seasons in ChampCar history. He became the first driver in 32 years to win the first three races of the ChampCar season, earning front-row starts in all three: St. Petersburg, Monterey and Long Beach. He also became the first Canadian driver to win a ChampCar race on home soil—during the record-setting race in Toronto, he led throughout every lap and was so far ahead at one point that when the first full-course caution of the race came out, Tracy finished his pitstop before anyone else could even get close to the pit-stop entrance. By the end of the 2003 season, Tracy was in the top-five list of ChampCar all-time wins (26), poles (19), starts (209), laps led (3386) and wins from pole (8), and his ChampCar championship-winning total was enough to award Canada its first Nations Cup award—a Cup held previously for four seasons by Brazil. That year Tracy was also *RACER* magazine's Racer of the Year, as well as *SPEED* and WorldCom's most popular driver. He continued to race in ChampCar until 2007, but never had another season to rival 2003. One of Tracy's most recent races was in 2008 with Vision Racing/Walker Racing at the Rexall Edmonton Indy, where he finished fourth. As of 2009, the IndyCar team KV Racing Technology was in talks with Tracy, and it was also speculated that Tracy might be involved in the NASCAR Camping World Truck Series in the future.

Lionel Conacher Award

Each year the Canadian Press honours Canada's top male athlete with the Lionel Conacher Award. The prize is named after the late everyman Lionel Conacher, a Canadian star in football, hockey, lacrosse, baseball, boxing and wrestling.

Lionel Conacher Award Winners

Year	Athlete	Sport
2008	Justin Morneau	Baseball
2007	Sidney Crosby	Hockey
2006	Steve Nash	Basketball
2005	Steve Nash	Basketball
2004	Kyle Shewfelt	Gymnastics
2003	Mike Weir	Golf
2002	Steve Nash	Basketball
2001	Mike Weir	Golf
2000	Mike Weir	Golf
1999	Wayne Gretzky—Athlete of the Century	Hockey
1998	Larry Walker	Baseball
1997	Jacques Villeneuve	Auto Racing
1996	Donovan Bailey	Track and Field
1995	Jacques Villeneuve	Auto Racing
1994	Elvis Stojko	Figure Skating
1993	Mario Lemieux	Hockey
1992	Mark Tewksbury	Swimming
1991	Kurt Browning	Figure Skating
1990	Kurt Browning	Figure Skating
1989	Wayne Gretzky	Hockey
1988	Mario Lemieux	Hockey

Lionel Conacher cont.

Year	Athlete	Sport
1987	Ben Johnson	Track and Field
1986	Ben Johnson	Track and Field
1985	Wayne Gretzky	Hockey
1984	Alex Baumann	Swimming
1983	Wayne Gretzky	Hockey
1982	Wayne Gretzky	Hockey
1981	Wayne Gretzky	Hockey
1980	Wayne Gretzky	Hockey
1979	Gilles Villeneuve	Auto Racing
1978	Graham Smith	Swimming
1977	Guy Lafleur	Hockey
1976	Greg Joy	Track and Field
1975	Bobby Clarke	Hockey
1974	Ferguson Jenkins	Baseball
1973	Phil Esposito	Hockey
1972	Phil Esposito	Hockey
1971	Ferguson Jenkins	Baseball
1970	Bobby Orr	Hockey
1969	Russ Jackson	Football
1968	Ferguson Jenkins	Baseball
1967	Ferguson Jenkins	Baseball
1966	Bobby Hull	Hockey
1965	Bobby Hull	Hockey
1964	Bill Crothers	Track and Field
1963	Gordie Howe	Hockey
1962	Bruce Kidd	Track and Field
1961	Bruce Kidd	Track and Field
1960	Ron Stewart	Football
1959	Russ Jackson	Football
1958	Maurice Richard	Hockey

Lionel Conacher cont.

Year	Athlete	Sport
1957	Maurice Richard	Hockey
1956	Jean Beliveau	Hockey
1955	Normie Kwong	Football
1954	Rich Ferguson	Track and Field
1953	Doug Hepburn	Weightlifting
1952	Maurice Richard	Hockey
1951	No award given	—
1950	Lionel Conacher—Athlete of the Half Century	Football/Hockey
1949	Frank Filchock	Football
1948	Buddy O'Connor	Hockey
1947	Joe Krol	Football
1946	Joe Krol	Football
1945	No award because of World War II	—
1944	No award because of World War II	—
1943	No award because of World War II	—
1942	No award because of World War II	—
1941	Tony Golab	Football
1940	Gérard Côté	Track and Field
1939	Fritz Hanson	Football
1938	Hugh "Bummer" Stirling	Football
1937	Syl Apps	Hockey
1936	Phil Edwards	Track and Field
1935	Rober "Scotty" Rankine	Track and Field
1934	Harold Webster	Track and Field
1933	Dave Komonen	Track and Field
1932	Ross Somerville	Golf

Squash
Jonathon Power

The last name of this Comox, BC-born Canadian says it all. Beginning to play squash at age seven on the military base where his father worked, and turning professional at age 16 in 1990, Jonathon Power immediately became a force to be reckoned with. Based in Amsterdam at the start of his career and then training in Montréal in the latter half, Power reached levels of success unheard of for a Canadian squash player. Winner of 36 Professional Squash Association tournaments; the 1998 World Open; the 1999 British Open; the 2002 and 2003 Super Series Finals; the 2001, 2002 and 2005 PSA Masters; the 1996, 1999, 2000 and 2002 Tournament of Champions; and the men's singles gold medal at the 2002 Commonwealth Games, Power's statistics rarely listed defeats. Amid his many first-place finishes, Power became the first North American to reach the world number one ranking in squash, in 1999.

Dubbed "The Magician," Power's wide range of drop and deception shots were revered in the world of squash throughout his career. After making it to the top in 1999, he once again reached number one in 2006, marking the longest gap between periods of holding this position of any player in squash history. Power called his world number one rankings his greatest achievements, but was happy to have gotten where he did without following a mould: "I didn't have any mould or path to follow, no traditions to guide me. I had to figure it all out on my feet and on my own." Known as a colourful personality who often disputed with referees, the squash court became a lot more quiet in 2006, when shortly after achieving the world number one ranking for the second time, Power announced his retirement. Upon his declaration, it didn't take long for post-career accolades to start rolling in. In 2006, Power was inducted into Canada's Sports Hall of Fame (the first squash player to have this honour), and in 2007 was inducted into the Ontario Squash Hall of Fame. He also has a court named after him at his training club in Montréal, the Club Sportif MMA.

"My game has always been at top level, I never felt anyone was better than me," Power said after a tournament in 2005, but this was true of his entire career, as he remains the most successful North American squash player of all time.

Golf

Mike Weir

A Canadian would have to live under a rock to not know about some level of Mike Weir's success as a golfer. Born in Sarnia, Ontario, and growing up in nearby Bright's Grove, Weir is the first Canadian golfer to ever win a major title, and the distinction came at the end of golf's most celebrated event, The Masters, in 2003. However, this left-handed golfer's road to PGA Tour fame was not without its obstacles.

Turning pro in 1992, Weir was named the Canadian Tour Rookie of the Year in 1993 and tried to make the PGA Tour five times before he finally qualified. Within six years of becoming a professional, Weir was 131st on the PGA Tour money list in 1998 and won his first Tour title in 1999 at the Air Canada Championship in BC. His win there produced two further accomplishments for Weir: no Canadian golfer had won on native soil since 1954, and Canadian golfers had been completely absent from the Tour's winners' list since 1992.

Weir only improved from there on in, and he claimed the World Golf Championship in 2000, taking down opponents including Tiger Woods and Vijay Singh. Also in 2000, Weir became the first Canadian to play in the Presidents Cup and was subsequently awarded the Canadian Press Male Athlete of the Year Award. Weir made it into the top 10 in the world rankings with his win at the 2001 PGA Tour Championship. Continuing to excel internationally, his seminal year came in 2003 when he won his Masters title, claimed his fourth PGA Tour title, became the first Canadian to win three times in a season, was fifth on the money list with earnings over $4.8 million and earned a spot on the Presidents Cup International Team. Of his Masters win, Weir said, "It's something I have dreamed about for a long time and something I worked very hard for. I have a tough time putting it into words and doing it justice."

Over the next five years, Weir also became the second-winningest left-hander in PGA Tour history and one of only six players to win the Northern Trust Open in back-to-back seasons.

Currently ranked in the top 20 in the World Golf Rankings, Weir has spread his wings much farther than the golf course. In 2007 he was appointed to the Order of Canada, and in 2009 was named Canada's top male professional by the Golf Journalists Association of Canada. It was also announced in 2009 that Weir will be inducted into the Canadian Golf Hall of Fame, matching George Knudson for the most victories by inductees who have played on the PGA Tour. Weir also has his own golf course in Graven-hurst, Ontario, called Taboo Resort Golf and Spa, a golf-clothing line, a special RBC Mike Weir VISA Card that offers exclusive golf-related perks, a charity that supports causes related to children—The Mike Weir Foundation—and a wine brand. It was announced in 2008 that Weir is going to have a winery built in his name, making him the first Canadian celebrity to have an actual wine estate that people can visit. But Weir isn't finished yet: "I have so much that I still want to accomplish both on the course and in helping to continue to grow the game in Canada...."

Sandra Post

In 1968, at 20 years old, Sandra Post won the LPGA Championship, setting the record she held for 39 years as the youngest player to ever win an LPGA major title. Born in Oakville, Ontario, Post won the Canadian Junior Girl's Championship three times before deciding to turn pro in 1968, the year of her record-setting win. With this victory, Post defeated defending champion Kathy Whitworth, nailing down the first win in the tournament by a non-U.S. player and a rookie.

Post's amazing year in 1968 awarded her the LPGA's Rookie of the Year honour.

In the years between 1968 and 1983, Post won eight LPGA tournaments, had 20 second-place finishes, including one at the U.S. Women's Open, and won $746,714 in prize money. This was more than any Canadian professional athlete at the time—male or female—had ever won. Post was also second place on the LPGA money list in 1979, a position that reflected her success of winning unprecedented back-to-back Dinah Shore Tournaments (now known as the Kraft-Nabisco Championship) in 1978 and 1979. Post also took home the 1979 Lou Marsh Trophy for Canada's Athlete of the Year and her first of two consecutive Bobbie Rosenfeld Awards as Canada's top female athlete.

Post continued to play golf professionally until 1983, winning the West Virginia Classic in 1980 and the McDonald's Kids Classic in 1981, but nothing ever topped her 1979 season. She decided to retire in 1984, and has gone on to receive great accolades in Canada, and has sustained a successful career beyond playing competitively in the worlds of amateur and professional golf. In 1988, Post was inducted into Canada's Sports Hall of Fame and the Royal Canadian Golf Association Hall of Fame; in 1999 she was placed at number eight in a survey by the Canadian Press and Broadcast News of the top-10 female Canadian athletes of the 20th century, and in 2003 was honoured with an Order of Canada.

She is also the founder of the successful Sandra Post School of Golf in Caledon, Ontario, has commentated for CTV, ABC and TSN, captained the Nation's Cup teams in 1999 and 2000, executive edited *Women's World Golf* and, with Jazz Golf, designed a golf-club set that was made especially for women.

Record-breaking Fact

At 46 years old, George Lyon became the first Canadian and the last-ever Olympian to win a gold medal in the sport of golf. Lyon discovered the game of golf late in life, swinging his first club at the age of 37. Considered the underdog at the 1904 Olympics in St. Louis, Lyon defeated his 23-year-old American competitor in the final to win the gold medal. After the medal was placed around his neck, Lyon proceeded to walk around the clubhouse on his hands in celebration.

Basketball
Steve Nash

A Canadian in the NBA is rare, but Steve Nash has managed to create an ongoing successful career in this professional league as one of North America's most notable basketball players, with remarkable skill in playmaking, ball-handling and shooting. Born in Johannesburg, South Africa, Nash immigrated to Canada with his British family when he was only two years old. His family moved from Regina to Vancouver to Victoria, where they settled. Developing a passion for basketball throughout high school, Nash was awarded a scholarship for the 1992–93 season by Santa Clara University (SCU) in California after his coach sent letters on Nash's behalf to more than 30 American universities. His skill was immediately apparent, and he led the SCU Broncos team to the West Coast Conference title and into the 1993 NCAA Men's Division I Basketball Tournament—a tournament in which the Broncos hadn't played for five years. The team made the NCAA tournament again in the 1994–95 season, with Nash leading the way as Conference Player of the Year and league leader in scoring and assists. Nash first considered turning professional at the end of that season, but decided to wait until the end of the 1995–96 season to try his hand at the NBA.

Selected 15th overall by the Phoenix Suns in the first round of the 1996 NBA draft, Nash's first season as a professional was a slow one, but his time on the court increased in his second season, and he was ranked 13th in the league for three-point field-goal percentage. Nash expressed a desire to move to the Dallas Mavericks for the 1998–99 season, and with a strategic push from a friend who was the son of the Mavericks coach at the time, Nash was traded. His talents were put to use in Dallas, and he quickly became one of the best point guards in the league. With Nash heading the offence, the Mavericks earned their first playoff berth in more than 10 years in 2000–01. Building off the team's success in past seasons, Nash, along with his fellow "Big Three" teammates Dirk Nowitzki and Michael Finley, led Dallas to the Western Conference finals in 2002–03, only the second appearance in these finals in the team's history.

At the end of the 2003–04 season, "Kid Canada" Nash became a free agent and tried to negotiate a long-term contract with Mavericks owner Mark Cuban, but Nash's former team, the Phoenix Suns, put in an offer that was much more lucrative than what Cuban was putting on the bargaining table. Nash asked Cuban if he would top the Suns offer, but he would not. Nash signed with Phoenix.

The Suns' previous season before Nash arrived had been dismal, and with his arrival, the Phoenix coach decided to try a different tactic and implement Nash's style of up-tempo, quick play. The Suns went on to a 62–20 record and a points-per-game average of 110.4, the highest the team had seen in 10 years. Nash also beat out Shaquille O'Neal and was awarded the 2004–05 NBA MVP Award—a first in Canadian history and only the second time an international player had won MVP. Nash received the MVP award again in the 2005–06 season. He was also second to Magic Johnson for point guards receiving the MVP honour more than once, and was the third point guard in NBA history to earn the award twice in a row (behind Johnson and Michael Jordan). Nash also won the NBA All-Star Skills Challenge in 2005.

Following his streak of firsts and major successes, in 2006–07 Nash experienced another career milestone when he became the first person since Johnson in 1990–91 to average 18 points and 11 assists per game during the regular season; Nash also received the most votes to make the All-NBA first-team, and was joined by teammate Amar'e Stoudemire. No two teammates had been chosen for the first-team since O'Neal and Kobe Bryant in 2003–04.

At the end of the season in 2007–08, Nash further proved his skill with the third-best free-throw shooting average in league history, and a total of assists, assists per game and three-point field goals that ranked him in the top-20 players in NBA history.

Nash continues to play for Phoenix in 2009, but will become a free agent in 2010, sparking speculation in the media that he could be the next to follow former teammates Raja Bell and Boris Diaw into a trade with another team. Nash, however, is remaining tight-lipped: "I don't know. Like I said before about the 2010 speculation, it's so far away."

In between his successful seasons in the NBA, Nash was also selected as captain of the Canadian Olympic basketball team in 2000 at Sydney and for the qualifying team hoping to make it to the Athens Olympics in 2004. At Team Canada's Olympic run for the podium in 2000, Nash and his teammates made it as far as the quarter-finals, only to lose to France. After leaving the court in tears, Nash said later, "It hurts a lot. I feel like I let everybody down. We could have been in the championship game. We were good enough." In 2004, Canada missed the qualifying podium by one spot, and it was the last time Nash played for Team Canada.

Canada has always loved Nash, however, and he has mirrored that sentiment back at his native land despite his frustration at the Sydney Olympics and the Athens qualifier. "[Canadian values] feels like common sense to me," he said. In 2005 he received Canada's most prestigious basketball award, the Dr. James Naismith Award of Excellence, and in 2008, Nash was added to Canada's Walk of Fame, the only basketball player to have a spot on one of Toronto's most famous sidewalks.

Record-breaking Fact

At the inaugural Olympic men's basketball event at the 1936 Games in Berlin, the Canadian men took home the silver medal while basketball inventor (and Canadian) James Naismith and International Olympic Committee founder Pierre de Coubertin watched in the stands. The Canadians lost the gold-medal game to the American squad, and the silver was the only Olympic medal the Canadian men's basketball team has ever won.

Junior Hockey

For many Canadian amateur hockey players, before the NHL comes the Canadian Hockey

League. Seen as one of the world's most prominent precursors to the NHL, the 60-team CHL, established in 1975, is comprised of three smaller leagues—the Ontario Hockey League, the Québec Major Junior Hockey League and the Western Hockey League—that play each year to battle their way to the coveted Memorial Cup. Each May, from coast to coast, Canadians gather at home and in pubs to see who will be the winner of one of Canada's most celebrated trophies.

The number of CHL players drafted to the NHL after the end of the hockey season often represents at least half of the professional league's draft entrants, and anticipation at each year's announcements is high. In showcasing Canada's talent in the good old hockey game, below is a listing of CHL records, in which some very recognizable NHL names are found.

CHL Records

Record		Athlete	Year
Most goals in a game	8	Mathieu Benoit	1999
	8	Normand Aubin	1979
	8	Stephan Lebeau	1986
Most goals in a season	133	Mario Lemieux	1983–84
Most career goals	309	Mike Bossy	—
Most assists in a game	9	Andre Savard	1971
	9	Mike Kaszycki	1976
Most assists in a season	157	Pierre Larouche	1973–74

CHL Records cont.

Record		Athlete	Year
Most career assists	408	Patrice Lefebvre	—
Most points in a game	12	Andre Savard	1971
Most points in a season	282	Mario Lemieux	1983–84
Most career points	595	Patrice Lefebvre	—
Most short-handed goals in a season	14	Al Stewart	1983–84
Most power-play goals in a season	47	Jason Krywulak	1992–93
Longest goal-scoring streak	27	Pierre Larouche	1973–74
Longest point streak	61	Mario Lemieux	1983–84
Most game-winning goals	18	Pat LaFontaine	1982–83
Fastest 50 goals from beginning of season (in games)	27	Bill Derlago	1977–78
	27	Mario Lemieux	1983–84
Most goals by a rookie in a season	104	Pat LaFontaine	1982–83
Most assists by a rookie in a season	130	Pat LaFontaine	1982–83
Most points by a rookie in a season	234	Pat LaFontaine	1982–83
Most shutouts in a season	13	Kelly Guard	2003–04
	13	Bryan Bridges	2004–05
Most career shutouts	22	Tyson Sexsmith*	—

*Player still active in 2009

Hockey
Wayne Gretzky

A Brantford, Ontario-born native, Wayne Gretzky is the most famous NHL hockey player to ever live. So famous, revered and honoured in the hockey world is he that his jersey number (99) has been retired throughout the entire NHL. Baseball player Jackie Robinson is the only other person in all of major professional sport to have this honour.

Putting on skates at the age of two, Gretzky learned to play hockey on a backyard rink his father made for him. But his father Walter didn't flood the ice religiously for a simple game of shinny with his son—skating and puck-handling drills were regularly practiced on the rink that came to be known as "Wally's Coliseum." Gretzky joined his first hockey team at the age of six, a team that consisted of 10-year-olds. His placement on a team many skill levels above where he should have been developmentally was a precedent for Gretzky's career.

By age 13, Gretzky had scored over 1000 goals but was suffering the wrath of jealous parents and players in his hometown because of his enormous skill on the ice. At 14, his parents arranged for him to move to Toronto, where he started to play with the Junior B Toronto Nationals team. Only a year later, at the age of 15, Gretzky signed with his first agent. Soon he was playing with the higher-level Ontario Midget Junior Hockey League. In only one year with the OMJHL, he broke the single-season scoring record and was later selected to play for Canada at the 1978 World Junior Championships. The youngest player there, he was the top scorer and named the best forward. Gretzky was next drafted to the CHL Sault Ste. Marie Greyhounds in Sault Ste. Marie, Ontario, and it was with the Greyhounds that he first wore 99 as his jersey number.

There was no doubt by this point that Gretzky was ready for the NHL, but the league did not allow the signing of players under the age of 20. So Gretzky signed with the Indianapolis Racers of the World Hockey League instead, a league that played in direct competition with the NHL. The Racers franchise started to go under shortly after Gretzky joined, and he soon ended up in Edmonton with the more successful then-WHL Oilers. At the age of 18 in 1979, Gretzky signed a 10-year personal services contract with Edmonton that was the longest in hockey history at the time. The Oilers ended up as one of the teams to survive the eventual demise of the WHL and become an NHL team, and it was in their first NHL season of 1979–80 that Gretzky debuted with the league, despite his age.

He began his NHL career with a bang, voted Most Valuable Player and tied for the scoring lead in his first year of NHL competition. Gretzky was also the youngest player at the time to have scored 50 goals in a season. In his second season in the NHL, he broke Bobby Orr's record for assists in a season, as well as Phil Esposito's for points in a season. Gretzky was just warming up: in the 1981–82 season, he broke Maurice Richard's 35-year-long record for 50 goals in 50 games by reaching 50 goals in only 39 games in a matchup against the Philadelphia Flyers. Afterwards, Flyers team captain Bobby Clarke went into the Oilers dressing room and told Gretzky, "I know everything that's been written about you. I think none of it is adequate."

That year, Gretzky also became the first and only player in league history to break the 200-point mark in a single season. Named the Associated Press Male Athlete of the Year, he became the first hockey player and first Canadian to ever achieve that honour. In following seasons and by the end of Gretzky's career in Edmonton, he held or shared 49 NHL records—a record in itself.

Captain of the Oilers from 1983–88, Gretzky led his team to four Stanley Cup wins. His career with Edmonton ended after the last Cup win in 1988, when Gretzky found out from his father that Oilers owner Peter Pocklington wanted to trade him. After all was said and done, Gretzky ended up with the Los Angeles Kings in a deal that was finalized when Gretzky called Pocklington to officially request the trade. Canada was not happy with Pocklington for allowing the trade to happen, and Canadians called Gretzky a traitor for leaving his country. Edmonton, however, never grew tired of him, and in Gretzky's first game back in the Oilers arena as a King, the attendance was the largest ever documented in Northlands Coliseum (now Rexall Place) history. Gretzky later commented, "I'm still proud to be a Canadian. I didn't desert my country...I'm Canadian to the core. I hope Canadians understand that."

Gretzky with Los Angeles was something to behold, much like every other hockey season he played. He was captain for his entire tenure with the Kings and was awarded the Male Athlete of the Decade honour by The Associated Press in 1990. Out with a back injury in the 1992–93 regular season, it was the one year Gretzky failed to lead his team in scoring. But that didn't matter as that season he broke Gordie Howe's NHL career goal-scoring record. In the years following, the Kings slipped in skill, and Gretzky eventually requested a trade, landing him with the Blues in St. Louis in 1996. Things didn't work out in St. Louis, and Gretzky signed with the

New York Rangers later in the year, where he would end his career as a player in the NHL.

On the Rangers bench for three seasons, Gretzky was named the number one greatest player in NHL history by *The Hockey News* in 1997. He was also part of Team Canada at the 1998 Nagano Olympics, and in the 1998–99 season broke Howe's professional (WHL and NHL) total goal-scoring record of 1071. This was Gretzky's last season in the NHL, and he announced his retirement in 1999. He played his last game against the Pittsburgh Penguins at Madison Square Garden and said years later:

> *My last game in New York was my greatest day in hockey…looking in the stands and seeing your mom and dad and your friends, that all came together in that last game in New York.*

The same year he retired, Gretzky was inducted into the Hockey Hall of Fame and had a highway named after him in Edmonton. In 2000, he was made a member of the International Ice Hockey Federation Hall of Fame. Since 1999, Gretzky has become involved in all facets of hockey, never removing himself from the sport. He eventually took the position as head coach of the Phoenix Coyotes from 2005 to 2009, was named the executive director for Canada's 2002 and 2006 men's

Olympic hockey teams and played in the 2003 Heritage Classic in Edmonton.

Following his father's mantra of "Don't go where the puck was, go where the puck is going to be," Gretzky played an unparalleled career in the NHL, holding or sharing 61 records in the league, proving there is no doubt as to why he is "The Great One" to Canada as well as the world.

Wayne Gretzky's Records

- **Most Career Points:**
    2856 (1485 games, 894 goals, 1962 assists)
- **Most Career Points (including playoffs):**
    3238 (2856 in the regular season and 382 in the playoffs)
- **Most Goals:**
    894
- **Most Goals (including playoffs):**
    1016 (894 in the regular season and 122 in the playoffs)
- **Most Assists:**
    1962
- **Most Assists (including playoffs):**
    2222 (1962 in the regular season and 260 in the playoffs)
- **Most Goals by a Centre:**
    894
- **Most Assists by a Centre:**
    1962
- **Most Points by a Centre:**
    2856
- **Most 40-or-more Goal Seasons:**
    12

- **Most Consecutive 40-or-more Goal Seasons:**
  12

- **Most 50-or-more Goal Seasons:**
  9 (tied with Mike Bossy)

- **Most 60-or-more Goal Seasons:**
  5 (tied with Mike Bossy)

- **Most Consecutive 60-or-more Goal Seasons:**
  4 (1981–82 to 1984–85)

- **Most 100-or-more Point Seasons:**
  15

- **Most Consecutive 100-or-more Point Seasons:**
  13 (1979–80 to 1991–92)

- **Most three-or-more Goal Games:**
  50 (37 three-goal games; 9 four-goal games; 4 five-goal games)

- **Most Overtime Assists:**
  15

- **Highest Assists-per-Game Average:**
  1.321 (1962 assists in 1485 games)

- **Most Points in One Season:**
  215 (1985–86 with an 80-game schedule)

- **Most Points in One Season (including playoffs):**
  255 (1984–85; 208 points in 80 regular-season games and 47 points in 18 playoff games)

- **Most Goals in One Season:**
  92 (1981–82 with an 80-game schedule)

- **Most Goals in One Season (including playoffs):**
  100 (1983–84; 87 goals in 74 regular-season games and 13 goals in 19 playoff games)

- **Most Goals in 50 Games from Start of Season:**
  61 (1981–82 and 1983–84)

- **Most Assists in One Season:**
  163 (1985–86 with an 80-game schedule)

- **Most Assists in One Season (including playoffs):**
  174 (1985–86; 163 assists in 80 regular-season games and 11 assists in 10 playoff games)

- **Most Points by a Centre in One Season:**
  215 (1985–86 with an 80-game schedule)

- **Most Goals by a Centre in One Season:**
  92 (1981–82 with an 80-game schedule)

- **Most Assists by a Centre in One Season:**
  163 (1985–86 with an 80-game schedule)

- **Most three-or-more Goal Games in One Season:**
  10 (1981–82; 6 three-goal games; 3 four-goal games; 1 five-goal game)

- **Longest Consecutive Assist-scoring Streak:**
  23 games: 48 assists (1990–91)

- **Longest Consecutive Point-scoring Streak:**
  51 games: 61 goals, 92 assists for 153 points (October 5, 1983, to January 28, 1984)

- **Longest Consecutive Point-scoring Streak from Start of Season:**
  51 games: 61 goals, 92 assists for 153 points

- **Highest Goals per Game Average in One Season:**
  1.18 (1983–84; 87 goals in 74 games)

- **Highest Assists per Game Average in One Season:**
  2.04 (1985–86; 163 assists in 80 games)

- **Highest Points per Game Average in One Season:**
  2.77 (1983–84; 205 points in 74 games)

- **Most Goals in One Period:**
  4 (tied with 10 other players)

- **Most Assists in One Game:**
  7 (tied with Billy Taylor)

- **Most Assists in One Road Game:**
  7 (tied with Billy Taylor)

- **Most Assists in One Game by a Player in his First NHL Season:**
  7 on February 15, 1980

- **Most Career Playoff Goals:**
  122

- **Most Career Playoff Assists:**
  260
- **Most Career Playoff Points:**
  382 (122 goals and 260 assists)
- **Most Career Game-winning Goals in the Playoffs:**
  24
- **Most three-or-more Goal Games in the Playoffs:**
  10 (8 three-goal games, 2 four-goal games)
- **Most Points in One Playoff Year:**
  47 (1985; 17 goals and 30 assists in 18 games)
- **Most Assists in One Playoff Year:**
  31 (1988; 19 games)
- **Most Points in a Stanley Cup Final:**
  13 (1988; 3 goals and 10 assists)
- **Most Assists in a Stanley Cup Final:**
  10 (1988)
- **Most Assists in a Playoff Series (excluding the Stanley Cup finals):**
  14 (1985; Conference finals, 6 games vs. Chicago)
- **Most Short-handed Goals in One Playoff Year:**
  3 (tied with 5 other players)
- **Most Assists in One Playoff Game:**
  6 (April 9, 1987, at Edmonton; tied with Mikko Leinonen)
- **Most Points in One Playoff Period:**
  4 (April 12, 1987: 1 goal, 3 assists; tied with 9 other players)
- **Most Assists in One Playoff Period:**
  3 (This has been accomplished 5 times by Gretzky and 70 times league-wide)
- **Most Short-handed Goals in One Playoff Game:**
  2 (April 6, 1983, at Edmonton; tied with 8 other players)
- **Most All-Star Game Goals:**
  13 (in 18 games played)
- **Most All-Star Game Goals in One Game:**
  4 (1983 Campbell Conference; tied with 3 other players)
- **Most All-Star Game Goals in One Period:**
  4 (1983 Campbell Conference in the third period)

- **Most All-Star Game Points in One Period:**
  4 (1983 Campbell Conference in the third period; tied with Mike Gartner and Adam Oates)
- **Most Career All-Star Game Points:**
  25 (13 goals and 12 assists in 18 games)
- **Most Career All-Star Game Assists:**
  12 (tied with 4 players)

Gordie Howe

The third-best player in the history of the NHL, as voted by *The Hockey News*, Gordie Howe is a hero in the hockey world and the only player to have competed in the NHL in five different decades. Born in 1928 in Floral, Saskatchewan, Howe's family later moved to Saskatoon, his hometown, where he got his start in hockey. He left the city at age 16 when he was signed with the Detroit Red Wings to play for their junior team in Galt, Ontario. But, because of the team's tendency to favour the development of its older players, Howe did not get a lot of ice time and was promoted to the Omaha Knights in the United States Hockey League in lieu of staying on in Galt.

Not long after this promotion, Howe played his first game in the NHL at age 18 in 1946 with the Red Wings. His skill as a right-winger was immediately apparent, as was his propensity for fighting. "If a guy slashed me, I'd grab his stick, pull him up alongside me and elbow him in the head," Howe has said.

Only two seasons after his debut in the NHL, Howe led his team to first place in the regular season and did so for seven years in a row, a record yet to be broken by another NHL team. He also won four Stanley Cups with the Red Wings and steadily rose in the ranks of leading scorers in the league. During the 1950s, Howe entertained a friendly rivalry with fellow NHLer Maurice Richard, fuelled by fan comparisons more than anything else. Richard, who played for the Montréal Canadiens and was also a right-winger who wore the number 9 on his jersey, was one of Howe's top competitors for lead scorer and wasn't afraid to fight when necessary. In the four Stanley Cups Howe won with the Red Wings, each final was played against Richard and the Canadiens.

In the late sixties, the NHL expanded to 12 teams from 6, and in its augural season as a larger league (1967–68), Howe reached 100 points— the only time he did so in his career, with 44 goals and 59 assists—ending the season at 103 points. By now, Howe was 40 years old and for most players, the end of their time in the NHL as a player would have been near. He played two more seasons with the Red Wings and retired in 1971 because of a chronic wrist injury. He stayed in Detroit, working in the Red Wings front office, but left a year later after feeling underutilized in his position. Offered a contract by the World Hockey League Houston Astros (a team that Howe's two sons had signed with as well), he had wrist surgery in order to make his return to the ice. He did so with great success, leading his team, in his late forties, to back-to-back championships and earning the Gary L. Davidson Trophy in 1974 as the WHL's MVP.

The WHL met its end 1979, the same year the Hartford Whalers became part of the NHL. At age 51, Howe signed with the Whalers and played every game of 80 in his last season in the NHL. Selected to play in the All-Star game that season, Howe skated beside a young 19-year-old Wayne Gretzky. At the end of Howe's career, he ranked first in career regular-season goals with 975 (combining his seasons in the NHL and WHL), a record Gretzky later surpassed. Howe remains at the top of the list for total games played (1767), throughout his career became known as Mr. Hockey and finished in the top five in scoring for 20 seasons in a row, an accomplishment never reached by any other athlete in any sport.

In 1997, Howe took to the ice one more time, signing a one-game contract with the International Hockey League Detroit Vipers. He skated one shift on the ice while the crowd watched this remarkable 70-year-old who just couldn't quit the game. Howe has been awarded almost every accolade there is for an NHL player and Canadian. He has a place in the Hockey Hall of Fame, Canada's Sports Hall of Fame and Canada's Walk of Fame, was the first-time recipient of the NHL Lifetime Achievement Award and is a member of the Order of Canada. According to former Red Wings coach Jack Adams, "There is Gordie Howe and there are other hockey players who are merely great."

Bobby Orr

Considered by many to be one of the other top hockey players to ever skate in the NHL, Bobby Orr remains the only defenceman to have won the league's scoring title, with two Art Ross trophies to his name. Orr also calls himself the owner of the record for most points and assists in a single season by a defenceman—not too bad for a small-town Parry Sound, Ontario, boy.

Orr got his start in hockey at the age of four, and it was as a bantam-age player that the Boston Bruins discovered him in Ontario. Boston invested in Orr's team, earning their rights to him as a player, and Orr suddenly found himself playing for the Oshawa Generals as a 14-year-old in a junior league that consisted of players who were 18, 19 and 20. Orr played with the Generals until he was 18 and old enough to enter the NHL.

His first contract with the Bruins was for $25,000, making Orr the highest-paid player in league history at the time (1966).

Winner of the Calder Memorial Trophy for the NHL's most outstanding rookie in his debut season with the Bruins, Orr won his first Norris Trophy as the league's best defenceman in 1968, despite being injured and only playing half the season. His prowess on the ice only grew in the following years, and in the 1969–70 Stanley Cup playoffs, Orr scored the final goal in overtime to win the game, awarding the Bruins their first Cup in 29 years. Orr said:

> *I never thought there could be such a day. This is what every kid dreams of, scoring the winning goal in a Stanley Cup overtime final. Wow! I can't find words to express what I feel.*

Orr was just warming up, however, and in 1971 he set records that haven't been broken yet for points in a season by a defenceman and for highest plus/minus (+124) by any position player. He once again scored the winning goal in the 1972 Stanley Cup Championship, and led the Bruins to another Cup final in 1974 where they lost against the Philadelphia Flyers.

In 1976, still with the Bruins as a free agent, they offered him an extended contract that would give him an 18-percent ownership of the Bruins franchise. It is believed in the hockey world that Orr's original contract lawyer from 1966, Alan Eagleson, kept this proposal from Orr, urging him to sign with the Chicago Blackhawks who were supposedly offering a better deal. Eagleson's disclosure of the deal, however, was printed in newspapers just days before Orr signed with the Blackhawks, which is where the debate has raged over the decades. Who knew what when?

It was discovered several years later that Eagleson had more than comfortable relations with Chicago owner Bill Wirtz and often colluded with owners in order to keep salaries down. Eagleson was later convicted in both Canada and the U.S. for keeping information from his clients and pilfering from the NHL Players Association (NHLPA) pension fund.

So, whether or not Orr really knew the whole story in 1976 is still up in the air, but the fact that he played with the Blackhawks for the late seventies is indisputable. Unfortunately plagued by injuries that persisted throughout much of his career, Orr ended up playing a meagre 26 games in three seasons in Chicago. In 1979, he retired. His storied career in the NHL included becoming the only player in the history of the NHL to win four major NHL awards in one season (the James Norris Memorial Trophy, the Art Ross Trophy, the Hart Memorial Trophy and the Conn Smythe Trophy), and the only NHLer to ever win the Norris trophy eight times.

Orr expressed no regrets about his unusually aggressive style as a defenceman that cost him his knees and, ultimately, his career.

It was the way I played. I liked to carry the puck and if you do that, you're going to get hit. I wish I'd played longer, but I don't regret it. I had a style— when you play, you play all-out. I tried to do things. I didn't want to sit back. I wanted to be involved.

The three-year waiting period for induction into the Hockey Hall of Fame was waived for Orr, and in 1979 he became a member, the youngest player to ever be included in this exclusive club. Also that year, Orr's jersey (number 4) was retired in Boston, and during the ceremony he said, "I spent ten years here and they were the ten best years of my life!"

Orr also has his own hall of fame in Parry Sound and a star on Canada's Walk of Fame. In the new millennium, Orr has worked as an agent to young hockey hopefuls through his player agency the Orr Hockey Group.

Dave Williams

Dave Williams, or as more commonly known, "Tiger" Williams, was born in Weyburn, Saskatchewan, and eventually became known as one of the toughest players in the NHL, breaking many penalty-minute league and club records in the process. Williams received his nickname from his hockey coach when he was five years old, and the name stuck throughout his entire amateur and professional hockey career.

Drafted into the professional leagues by both the Toronto Maple Leafs of the NHL and the Cincinnati Stringers of the WHL in 1974, Williams chose to play with the Leafs, where he stayed until 1980 and later said was the best place to play hockey in the world. He was at the top of the league in penalty minutes twice in his tenure in Toronto, with 338 in the 1976–77 season and 298 in the 1978–79 season. However, Williams wasn't just about roughing up his opponents, and was a well-rounded player with a good scoring record who entertained fans by riding his hockey stick down the entire length of the ice after he scored a goal.

Traded to the Vancouver Canucks in the middle of the 1979–80 season, Williams again led the league in penalty minutes in 1980–81, with 343 in 77 games. That year he was also the team leader in goals scored, with 35. The beginning of the 1984–85 season saw Williams with the Detroit Red Wings, but he was traded to the Los Angeles Kings later in the year. It was with the Kings that he set his career-high record of 358 penalty minutes in one season. Williams played with Los Angeles until 1987–88 when he was traded to the Hartford Whalers. This was his last season in the NHL, and he retired in 1988 with the most NHL career regular-season penalty minutes (3966), and most NHL career penalty minutes, including the regular season and playoffs, with 4421. He also holds a total of five records between the Maple Leafs and Canucks, all in penalty-minute categories.

Martin Brodeur

Born in Montréal, Québec, in 1972, Martin Brodeur is a goalie who has spent his entire NHL career with the New Jersey Devils. As of 2009, he held more than 30 records within his franchise and was second in NHL history for all-time wins and all-time shutouts. Brodeur's father was an Olympic goalie and, later, a photographer for the Montréal Canadiens, which was how Brodeur was introduced to the hockey rink. Growing up idolizing Montréal goalie Patrick Roy, Brodeur didn't play in goal himself until his minor hockey coach gave him the choice of starting the season as the forward he normally was, or giving the goaltender position a try. This proved to be a turning point in the young career of Brodeur.

Sticking with goaltending, in 1990 at the age of 18, Brodeur made it into the Québec Major Junior Hockey League, and in the same year was drafted in the first round, 20th overall, by the New Jersey Devils. He made his NHL debut in the 1991–92 season, but played only five games in total. For the next year and a half, Brodeur played with the Utica Devils of the American Hockey League before getting called up again to the Devils in 1994. It was in this year that Brodeur had his breakout season in the NHL, leading his team to the second-best record in the league and the Conference finals in the playoffs. Thanks to his efforts in net that season, he was awarded the Calder Memorial Trophy.

In the 1994–95 hockey season, the Devils won the first Stanley Cup in the club's history, led to a victory by Brodeur after many thought earlier in the season that New Jersey had no chance of becoming a Cup contender. In ousting the Detroit Red Wings for the Stanley Cup that year, Brodeur said after the last game:

> ...the time from ten minutes left to one minute left was probably the longest nine minutes of my life. But from one to zero was probably the greatest

time I've ever had. I didn't want the clock to run
out. It was such a great feeling: people crying in
the stands, people jumping up and down, people
cheering. Guys couldn't even sit up on the bench. It
was probably the best minute of my life.

Brodeur, in an interview on *Hockey Night in Canada* 13 years after this Cup series, admitted he experienced his most memorable save, against Red Wing Kris Draper.

Brodeur continued his success after the 1994–95 season, setting a record for most minutes played by a goalie in a single season in 1995–96, and in 1997 becoming only the second goalie in NHL history to score a goal in the playoffs. He also led the league with the lowest goals-against average in nearly 30 years of NHL history.

In the 1999–2000 season, Brodeur was the star in goal prevention, leading his team to another Stanley Cup win after they were once again largely considered the underdog. Riding high on his skills in the net, Brodeur played every game except the opener at the 2002 Salt Lake City Olympics, where Team Canada won the gold over the U.S. in the final.

Coming back from this victory and heading into the 2002–03 hockey season, Brodeur led the Devils to their third Cup. Between 2002 and 2003, Brodeur performed spectacularly, taking home the Vezina Trophy (his first of four) for being the league's top goaltender, his third William M. Jennings Trophy for playing a minimum of 25 games with the fewest goals-against in the league, becoming a finalist in the running for the Hart Memorial Trophy for MVP and experiencing the All-Star team as a First Team All-Star.

Never leaving New Jersey, Brodeur signed a contract extension with the team in 2006 that will see him stay with the Devils until 2012. Between 2006 and 2009, Brodeur passed his childhood idol Roy by claiming the all-time lead in overtime (non-shootout) wins (45), setting a league record for most consecutive wins for a team (38) and breaking the NHL record for most wins in a single season (48). In Brodeur's career to date, he is the youngest player in NHL history to attain the 300, 400 and 500 regular-season win marks (with his 400th win pinning him as the first goaltender to win that many games playing for the same team).

Brodeur hopes to compete as the starting goalie for Team Canada at the Vancouver 2010 Olympics. He said in an interview with the *Toronto Star*:

> *Playing for Canada changed my career* [referring to his gold at Salt Lake City in 2002]. *I want to have the chance to start, to be the guy again. I'm willing to go toe-to-toe with anyone. Competition, for me, is healthy.*

NHL Records

Record		Athlete	Year
Most goals in a season	92	Wayne Gretzky	1981–82
Most goals in a game	7	Joe Malone	1919–20
Most career goals	894	Wayne Gretzky	—
Most assists in a season	163	Wayne Gretzky	1985–86
Most assists in a game	7	Billy Taylor	1946–47
	7	Wayne Gretzky	1980, 1985, 1986
Most career assists	1963	Wayne Gretzky	—
Most point in a season	215	Wayne Gretzky	1985–86
Most points in a game	10	Darryl Sittler	1975–76
Most career points	2857	Wayne Gretzky	—
Most career games played	1767	Gordie Howe	—
Most wins in a season	48	Martin Brodeur	2006–07
Most career wins	551	Patrick Roy	—
Lowest goals-against average in a season	0.92	George Hainsworth	1928–29
Lowest career goals-against average	1.911	George Hainsworth	—
Most shutouts in a season	22	George Hainsworth	1928–29
Most career shutouts		Terry Sawchuk	103
Most penalty minutes in a game	67	Randy Holt	1978–79
Most penalty minutes in a season	472	Dave Schultz	1974–75
Most career penalty minutes	3966	Dave Williams	—
Most goals in a playoff game	5	Newsy Lalonde	1919
	5	Maurice Richard	1944
	5	Darryl Sittler	1976
	5	Reggie Leach	1976
	5	Mario Lemieux	1989
Most playoff goals in a season	19	Reggie Leach	1976
	19	Jari Kurri	1985

NHL Records cont.

Record		Athlete	Year
Most career playoff goals	122	Wayne Gretzky	—
Most assists in a playoff game	6	Mikko Leinonen	1982
	6	Wayne Gretzky	1987
Most playoff assists in a season	31	Wayne Gretzky	1988
Most career playoff assists	260	Wayne Gretzky	—
Most points in a playoff game	8	Patrick Sundstrom	1988
	8	Mario Lemieux	1989
Most playoff points in a season	47	Wayne Gretzky	1985
Most career playoff points	382	Wayne Gretzky	—
Most career playoff wins	151	Patrick Roy	—
Most playoff shutouts in a season	7	Martin Brodeur	2003
Most career playoff shutouts	22	Martin Brodeur	—
	22	Patrick Roy	—
Most trophies won in a season	4	Bobby Orr	1969–70
Most career trophies won	26	Wayne Gretzky	—
Most career games coached	2141	Scotty Bowman	—
Most career wins as a coach	1244	Scotty Bowman	—
Most Stanley Cup wins as a coach	9	Scotty Bowman	—

Notes on Sources

Alison Sydor. www.canoe.ca/2000GamesBiosN2Z/sydor.html

Barbara Scott. www.womenshistory.about.com/od/figureskaters/p/barbara_scott.htm

Bobby Orr. www.legendsofhockey.net/html/spot_oneononep197902.htm

Canadian Football League. www.cfl.ca/page/stats_indrec_rushing

Catriona Le May-Doan. www.catrionalemaydoan.ca/

Cindy Klassen. www.cindyklassen.com/biography.htm

Cindy Klassen. blog.macleans.ca/2008/12/08/cindy-klassen-sits-out-the-skating-season—on-a-bike/

Dave Williams. www.oldtimershockey.com/players/williams.html

Denny Morrison. www.denny-morrison.com/inthespotlight.htm

Elvis Stojko. www.elvisstojko.net/bio.html

George Reed. www.cfl.ca/page/his_legends_reed

Gilles Villeneuve. www.ferrariworld.com/events/villeneuve/home.html

Gilles Villeneuve. www.museegillesvilleneuve.com/english/.html

Jacques Villeneuve. www.askmen.com/celebs/men/sports/50_jacques_villeneuve.html

Jeremy Wotherspoon. www.speedskating-online.com/wotherspoon-march2007.htm

Jocelyn Lovell. www.etobicokesports.ca/lovell.html

Jonathon Power. www.jpsquash.com/jpsquash/

Kurt Browning. www.canadaswalkoffame.com/inductee/kurt-browning

Lennox Lewis. www.lennoxlewis.com/lennox/

Lennox Lewis. www.hbo.com/boxing/fighters/lewis_lennox/bio.html

Mike Weir. www.mikeweir.com/home/default.sps

Paul Tracy. www.paultracy.com/pt_profile.html

Sam Langford. www.blackhistorysociety.ca/SamLangford.htm

Sandra Post. www.sandrapost.ca/

Steve Bauer. www.stevebauer.com/bauerpower/aboutsteve/steve_bauer_bio.pdf

Steve Nash. www.bballcity.com/steve-nash-named-mvp/

Wayne Gretzky. www.nhl.com/history/gretzky.html